Secret London

Exploring the Hidden City, with Original Walks and Unusual Places to Visit

ANDREW DUNCAN

Interlink Books

An imprint of Interlink Publishing Group, Inc.
Northampton

This American edition first published 2006 by

INTERLINK BOOKS
An imprint of Interlink Publishing Group, Inc.
46 Crosby Street, Northampton, Massachusetts 01060
www.interlinkbooks.com

ISBN 1-56656-636-3

Reproduction by Pica Digital (Pte) Ltd, Singapore
Printed and bound in Singapore by Kyodo Printing Co (Singapore) Pte Ltd

Front cover: Kynance Mews, Kensington; Spine: Horse Guard, Whitehall;
Back cover: Italian fountains and pump house, Hyde Park (all Caroline Jones)

To request our complete 40-page full-color catalog,
please call us toll free at **1-800-238-LINK,** visit our website at **www.interlinkbooks.com**, or write to
Interlink Publishing
46 Crosby Street, Northampton, MA 01060
e-mail: sales@interlinkbooks.com

CONTENTS

MAPS

Key to Maps	
▬▬▬	Route of walk
⊖	Underground station
⇌	Railway station
🚻	Public toilets
⤙	Viewpoint
All maps are drawn on a north-south axis unless otherwise indicated.	

Note: Place and other names in the text printed in **bold type** have an entry in the Opening Times, Addresses and Other Information section beginning on page 177.

INTRODUCTION

Any city of six and a half million people is bound to be a very public place. But London also has its private side, a part that is deliberately kept covered up against prying eyes, or that is simply invisible because it is behind the scenes in some way. It's this private, this secret, side of London that is explored in this book.

In a place as big, as old and as multifaceted as London there are naturally many things that can be described as secret in one way or another. On the one hand there are things that are purposefully concealed, such as the locations of our secret service headquarters or the identities of publicity-shy aristocratic landowners. On the other hand there are things that are secret simply because the vast majority of people do not know about them. Here one might mention the natural landscape buried beneath London's streets and the true stories behind Dick Whittington and Marble Arch.

In uncovering these and other facets of secret London, my aim has been to penetrate as far as possible to the very heart of the city. One way I have tried to do this is by creating 20 miles of walks, revealing, among other things, the winding courses of three long-buried rivers. My other method has been to seek out new and unusual places to visit. Altogether, the book contains details of about 30 such places, including a roof garden in Kensington and a bell foundry in the East End.

In security-conscious Whitehall and Westminster I inevitably had less luck in pushing back the frontiers of public accessibility. However, I have at least been able to include in the book first-hand descriptions of some of the more historic government offices. I describe what goes on backstage in the Houses of Parliament and reveal how many people live there.

The one part of secret London I have not been able to explore is the extensive network of tunnels, sewers and abandoned tube stations that honeycombs the cold clay beneath the city's streets. However, by combining other researchers' findings with my own observations, I have been able to draw what I hope is a fairly complete outline of the subterranean city.

Any further light that readers can shed on this shadowy area and on any of the other aspects of secret London investigated in this book would be very welcome. Please e-mail your comments to me at andrew@andrewduncan.co.uk. For details of my other books visit my website at www.andrewduncan.co.uk.

Andrew Duncan

KEY TO MAPS CONTAINED IN THE BOOK

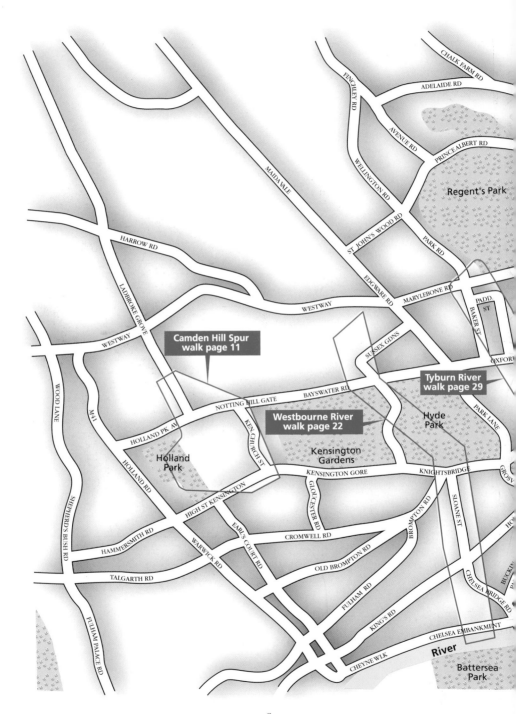

CHALK FARM RD

ADELAIDE RD

FINCHLEY RD

AVENUE RD

PRINCE ALBERT RD

WELLINGTON RD

Regent's Park

MAIDA VALE

ST JOHN'S WOOD RD

PARK RD

HARROW RD

EDGWARE RD

MARYLEBONE RD

PADD. ST

LADBROKE GROVE

WESTWAY

BAKER ST

WESTWAY

OXFORD

Camden Hill Spur walk page 11

SUSSEX GDNS

Tyburn River walk page 29

WOOD LANE

BAYSWATER RD

NOTTING HILL GATE

M41

KEN CHURCH ST

Westbourne River walk page 22

Hyde Park

PARK LANE

HOLLAND PK. AV

Kensington Gardens

Holland Park

HOLLAND RD

KENSINGTON GORE

KNIGHTSBRIDGE

GROSV

SHEPHERD'S BUSH RD

HIGH ST KENSINGTON

GLOUCESTER RD

BROMPTON RD

SLOANE ST

HO

HAMMERSMITH RD

EARL'S COURT RD

CROMWELL RD

WARWICK RD

OLD BROMPTON RD

TALGARTH RD

FULHAM RD

CHELSEA BRIDGE RD

BUCKI

FULHAM PALACE RD

KING'S RD

CHELSEA EMBANKMENT

P

CHEYNE WLK

River

Battersea Park

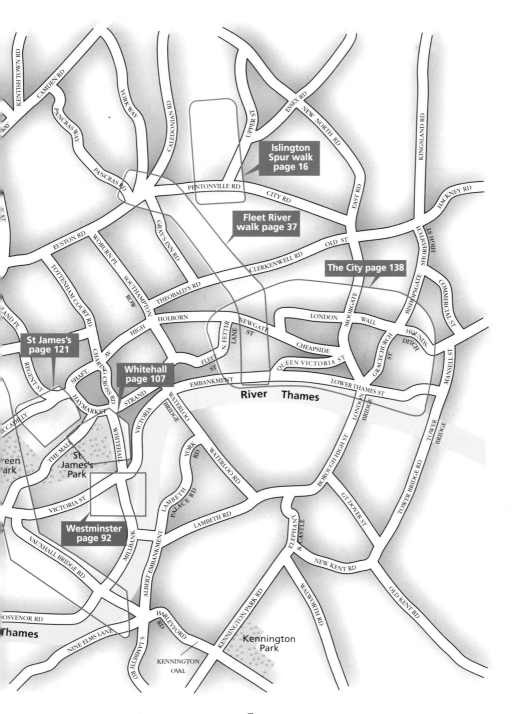

Islington
Spur walk
page 16

Fleet River
walk page 37

The City page 138

St James's
page 121

Whitehall
page 107

Westminster
page 92

KENTISH TOWN RD

CAMDEN RD

YORK WAY

PANCRAS WAY

CALEDONIAN RD

UPPER ST

ESSEX RD

NEW NORTH RD

KINGSLAND RD

HACKNEY RD

PANCRAS RD

PENTONVILLE RD

CITY RD

EAST RD

SHOREDITCH HIGH ST

EUSTON RD

WOBURN PL

GRAY'S INN RD

CLERKENWELL RD

OLD ST

COMMERCIAL ST

TOTTENHAM COURT RD

SOUTHAMPTON ROW

THEOBALD'S RD

LONDON WALL

BISHOPSGATE

MANSELL ST

HIGH HOLBORN

N. FETTER LANE

NEWGATE ST

MOORGATE

HOUNDS DITCH

CHEAPSIDE

GRACECHURCH ST

REGENT ST

SHAFT. AV.

CHARING CROSS RD

FLEET ST

QUEEN VICTORIA ST

HAYMARKET

STRAND

EMBANKMENT

LOWER THAMES ST

PICCADILLY

THE MALL

WHITEHALL

VICTORIA

WATERLOO BRIDGE

River   Thames

LONDON BRIDGE

TOWER BRIDGE

St
James's
Park

YORK RD

WATERLOO RD

BOROUGH HIGH ST

reen
ark

VICTORIA ST

LAMBETH PALACE RD

LAMBETH RD

GT DOVER ST

TOWER BRIDGE RD

MILLBANK

ALBERT EMBANKMENT

ELEPHANT & CASTLE

NEW KENT RD

OLD KENT RD

VAUXHALL BRIDGE RD

WALWORTH RD

OSVENOR RD

HARLEYFORD RD

KENNINGTON PARK RD

Kennington
Park

Thames

NINE ELMS LANE

LAMBETH RD

KENNINGTON
OVAL

HIDDEN LANDSCAPE

Beneath the streets of London lies a hidden landscape. Over the centuries it has been built on, covered up and generally obscured, but it is still very much in existence. Few Londoners are probably aware of it, even though it dictates things that affect their everyday lives, such as the layout of roads and streets, the position of important buildings and the routes of railways and canals, as well as less tangible things like boundaries and place names.

There's something about living in a city that seems to blind people to obvious geographical features that stand out in the countryside. Perhaps we just don't think about hills and valleys and streams when all we can see are endless vistas of bricks and mortar and tarmac. Travel is another factor: it is only when you provide your own motive power that you really become aware of ups and downs. That's why cyclists are usually the only ones who know where the ground rises and where it falls. But even they might find it difficult to say how the apparently unrelated humps and troughs on their regular routes fit into London's overall physical geography.

THE THAMES VALLEY

London's main geographical feature is of course the river valley in which it sits. The Thames valley is about 10 miles (16 kilometres) wide and 400 feet (120 metres) deep. One of the best places to see this is from Parliament Hill (319 feet; 97 metres) on Hampstead Heath.

It takes 20 minutes to walk there from Hampstead Underground Station (Northern Line) and the route is as follows. Turn left out of Hampstead Station and take the first left into Flask Walk. Follow the road (at first pedestrian only) down and to the right as far as the crossroads. Burgh House, Hampstead's community centre and local history museum, is on the left. Turn right into Willow Road and follow it down the hill to the junction with Downshire Hill. Here turn left, cross the main road and enter Hampstead Heath. Walk along the tarmac path with one of the Hampstead ponds – a source of the River Fleet (see page 37) – on your right. When you come to a track crossing left and right, go left and follow this main track round to the right between two more ponds. On the far side, follow the path up the hill, bending slightly right then left. When you come to a fork, go right (where it says 'No Cycling'). Soon you come out of the trees and, a minute later, reach the top of the hill.

View from Parliament Hill

Parliament Hill is not the highest spot in London, but it is higher than most and it commands extensive views east, south and south-west right across the valley, with the main landmarks to the south picked out on a panorama board. From this vantage point you can see that the city has slowly filled the bottom of the valley and then crept up and over the sides. You can also clearly see some of the features mentioned later. The first are the two valleys, one either side of the hill, from which flow the two streams that later come together to form the Fleet river. The second, to the left, is the long spur that starts up at Highgate and gently descends towards the City. A prominent landmark near the end of this spur is the former Caledonian market clocktower, which is visible when you step back and left from the panorama board about 10 paces.

At the bottom of the valley, the Thames meanders through its flood plain. Generally the plain is about 2 or 3 miles (3–5 kilometres) wide and less than 25 feet (7.5 metres) above sea level. To get an idea of its extent, take a map of London and draw a line south of the river from Greenwich to Putney. All the land between that line and the river is low flood plain. On the north bank, draw a line from Trafalgar Square to Hammersmith. Apart from a raised spit under Chelsea, all the land between that line and the river, including Westminster and Whitehall, is also flood plain.

Before it was drained, embanked and built on, the whole plain, especially on the south side, was subject to flooding. Indeed, in London's Roman era, Southwark and Lambeth, then tidal marsh (a modern street near Waterloo Station is even called Lower Marsh), were inundated with every high tide. Because south-east England is gradually sinking into the sea, the lowest parts of central London would still be subject to flooding were it not for the **Thames Barrier**.

THE TERRACES

Rising above the flood plain are two terraces, one at about 50 feet (15 metres) and the other at about 100 feet (30 metres). The terraces were caused by fluctuations in the volume of water flowing in the Thames. These fluctuations were in turn caused by variations in the speed at which local glaciers were melting. Millions of years ago the Thames flowed much further north than it does now. Then about 500,000 years ago the advancing glaciers of the Ice Age blocked the old river's drainage system, forcing it to seek a route further south. Starting 400 feet (120 metres) above where it is now, that is on a level with places like Hampstead and Highgate – which, though high ground now, were low ground then – it gradually wore its way down to its present level. For two eons during this gradual process, it flowed at relatively stable levels, hence the terraces. These are most evident on the river's north side where the flood plain gradually rises to the Northern Heights around Hampstead (440 feet; 134 metres) and Highgate (420 feet; 128 metres). On the south side, the plain rises more abruptly to places like Richmond, Wimbledon, Clapham Common, Forest Hill and Greenwich (with the first and last places – Richmond and Greenwich – being the closest hills to the river on the south side and thus the best places to go for river views).

The 50-foot terrace

In the West End and the City, the southern edge of the 50-foot terrace roughly follows a line along Piccadilly, the Strand, Fleet Street, Cannon Street and Eastcheap. From Piccadilly, walking west to east, you can see the ground steeply sloping to the right down Constitution Hill, Green Park and St James's (St James's Street and Duke Street St James's clearly show it). From the Strand, the slope is even more pronounced, but then one would expect that because the river, bending right at Charing Cross, has eaten into the hillside here, creating a sharp escarpment. The best places from which to view it are Waterloo Bridge and Adelphi Terrace. Further east, two good places to see the drop are Essex Street at the eastern end of the Strand and Dorset Rise at the eastern end of Fleet Street. Essex Street is built out on a sort of mound so that you have to go down a flight of steps at the end to descend to river level. The natural incline here is shown by adjacent Milford Lane. Dorset Rise climbs up from Tudor Street to Salisbury Square (see page 163). Dorset Buildings, leading off on the City side, ends in a vertical drop into the Fleet valley.

In the City, the brink of the terrace continues along St Paul's Churchyard, Cannon Street and Eastcheap. Take any right turn off these streets and you will find yourself plunging down to the river. Not surprisingly many of these side streets have the word 'hill' in their names: St Andrew's Hill, Addle Hill, White Lion Hill, Bennet's Hill, Lambeth Hill, Old Fish Street Hill, Huggin Hill, Garlick Hill, College Hill, Dowgate Hill, Laurence Pountney Hill, Fish Street Hill, St Mary-at- Hill and St Dunstan's Hill. The best place to view the slope is the top of the wide steps at Peters Hill leading down from **St Paul's Cathedral**.

The 100-foot terrace

The 100-foot terrace is a bit more difficult to explore than the lower terrace because it covers a much bigger area and is cut through by deeper and wider valleys. However, you can see it in the Islington area from the Primrose Hill viewpoint as described later (see pages 15–16). You also walk on it when you do the Campden Hill and Islington spur walks, described on the next page and on pages 16–21, respectively.

THE SPURS

The valleys just mentioned are the valleys of rivers running down from the Northern Heights to the Thames. There are seven rivers altogether. From west to east they are Stamford Brook, Counter's Creek, the Westbourne, the Tyburn, the Fleet, the Walbrook and the Lee. Four major spurs of high ground ending in more or less pronounced escarpments separate these rivers from each other and form prominent features of London's landscape.

The most westerly ends in two hills – Notting Hill (98 feet; 30 metres) and its higher neighbour, Campden Hill (124 feet; 38 metres) – which are the main features of our first spur walk.

THE CAMPDEN HILL SPUR WALK

Notting Hill and Campden Hill are two of London's most sought-after residential areas, in particular Notting Hill, where the designers of the Victorian Ladbroke estate included large communal gardens in their development. With all the trees in these gardens, and in Holland Park on Campden Hill, the views on the walk are somewhat restricted. However, the hilliness of the terrain and the variety of the architecture more than compensate.

Start:	Notting Hill Gate Underground (District, Circle and Central Lines).
Finish:	Kensington Underground (District and Circle Lines).
Length:	2½ miles (4 km).
Time:	1½ hours.
Refreshments:	The Windsor Castle pub, which serves better than average food and has a large walled beer garden, is at the half-way stage; towards the end of the walk there is a good café in Holland Park; otherwise there are plenty of places to eat and drink in Notting Hill Gate at the start of the walk and in Kensington High Street at the end.
Sights:	The Ladbroke estate, Holland Park and its **Ice House Gallery**, the **Commonwealth Institute**, Kensington High Street for shopping.
Note:	The views on this walk are in the western half of the compass, so it is best done in the morning with the sun behind you.

Come out of Notting Hill Gate Underground Station at the Notting Hill Gate north side/Portobello Road exit and walk straight on west across Pembridge Road and under the block of flats. Already you can see the ground dropping away to the west down Holland Park Avenue. At the end of the terrace of shops, just by the phone booth and traffic lights, turn right into an unnamed passage and continue straight on through the traffic barrier into Victoria Gardens. At the end turn left into Ladbroke Road.

Again, as the ground begins to drop away, turn right into Ladbroke Terrace and walk towards the private gardens in Ladbroke Square, the second largest in London and centrepiece of the Ladbroke estate. Turn left into the square. Once again, the ground ahead begins to fall away and in the far distance, framed by the trees, you can see the tops of blocks of flats nearly 2 miles (3 kilometres) away in Shepherd's Bush.

Notting Hill

The first road you come to is Ladbroke Grove. Turn right here and walk up the hill to the summit, marked by St John's Church with its landmark spire. This is Notting Hill. If you go a little way beyond the church to the brink of the hill on the north side, you can see down into Notting Dale with the Westway elevated motorway crossing Ladbroke Grove by the Underground station. This is where the annual Notting Hill carnival takes place in August. Beyond lies North Kensington and Kensal Town and, though you can't see it, the famous cemetery of Kensal Green, modelled on Père Lachaise in Paris.

Before the Ladbroke estate and the surrounding district were built up, from the 1840s onwards, Notting Hill was the central feature of a dramatically landscaped racecourse called the Hippodrome. Spectators watched from the summit where you are now, while the horses galloped round the circular course laid out around the base of the hill. For a while the course was a great success, but its long-term future was undermined by the exceptionally heavy going in Notting Dale, which was a menace to the horses. The Hippodrome closed in 1841, having been open for only four years. Crossing Ladbroke Grove, if you have not already done so, and returning to the church, turn right into Lansdowne Crescent. Now, as you follow the road round to the other end of the church, you see how the ground falls as steeply away to the west as it did to the north. The low ground at the bottom was drained by the stream called Counter's Creek before it was covered over and turned into a storm sewer.

Campden Hill

Once you have regained Ladbroke Grove, turn right and go back down the hill, keeping going until you reach Holland Park Avenue, the main road at

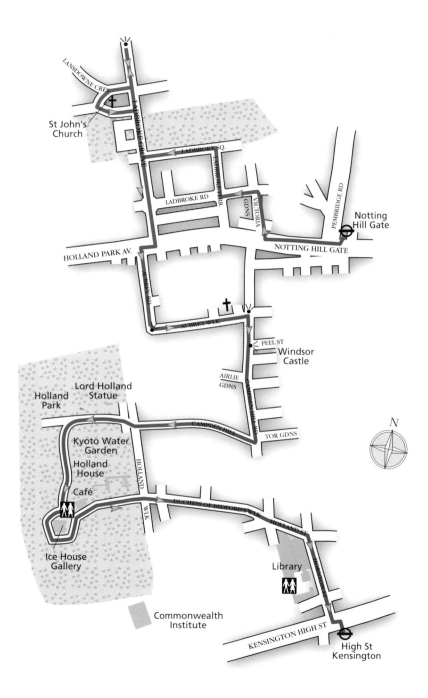

St John's
Church

LANSDOWNE CRES

LADBROKE GROVE

LADBROKE SQ.

LADBROKE RD.

LADBROKE PARK

VICTORIA GDNS

PEMBRIDGE RD

Notting
Hill Gate

NOTTING HILL GATE

HOLLAND PARK AV.

LADBROKE RD

AUBREY WLK

PEEL ST

Windsor
Castle

AIRLIE
GDNS

Lord Holland
Statue

Holland
Park

Kyoto Water
Garden

Holland
House

Café

CAMPDEN HILL

TOR GDNS

N

HOLLAND WLK

DUCHESS OF BEDFORD WK

HOLLAND ST

Ice House
Gallery

Library

Commonwealth
Institute

KENSINGTON HIGH ST

High St
Kensington

the end. Cross and turn right and then immediately left up the very steep Aubrey Road. Having descended Notting Hill, you are now climbing to the higher summit of Campden Hill. At the top of Aubrey Road, look back and you will see the tower and spire of St John's Church on the far side of what seems to be a valley filled with a dense mass of trees.

The big house just here is Aubrey House, named after Aubrey de Vere, one of Kensington's medieval lords of the manor. In the 18th century, when it had its own farm, Aubrey House was the home of the eccentric Lady Mary Coke, and there are many references to it in her diaries. All the farm and most of the extensive grounds have now been built on, but there is still a huge secret walled garden, completely invisible except from the south side of the house. Follow Aubrey Road round to the left where it becomes Aubrey Walk. To the right, new houses cover vast reservoirs that were built here in the mid 19th century by the Grand Junction Water Company. Looking left down Campden Hill Gardens, the top of a block of flats in Kensal Town called Trellick Tower comes into view. When you get to Campden Hill Road, the main road running over the hill, turn right and walk past the Windsor Castle pub, opened in 1837 when you could indeed see Windsor Castle from Campden Hill. As you look down Peel Street, next to the pub, the BT Tower, 3 miles (5 kilometres) away in the West End, punctures the horizon.

Holland Park

Beyond the Windsor Castle, you begin to descend the south side of Campden Hill. Carry on past Airlie Gardens and take the next right into Campden Hill. At the road end, continue on along the path that cuts through Holland Park School. Cross Holland Walk, go into Holland Park and turn right up the tarmac path.

Follow this path round to the left and go past the statue of the 3rd Lord Holland, to whose family this park once belonged. Now the ground falls steeply away again as you approach both the end of the Camden Hill spur and the western edge of Campden Hill and the 100-foot terrace. Although the thick foliage of the trees obscures the view at this point, the vista opens up a little at the first crossroads that you reach. Here turn left and walk past the Kyoto water garden, following the path round to the left where it is joined by another one coming up the hill. Then take the first right. This takes you on to the terrace in the formal garden area of the park. Walk along to the corner past the restaurant and art gallery. Although the trees are still quite thick, there are occasional glimpses of the long views west over the flat ground formerly drained by Counter's Creek and Stamford Brook. Turn left round the corner and walk through the colonnade out on to the broad walk that takes you in front of the remains of Holland House, a

17th-century mansion almost completely destroyed by bombs during the Second World War. (The grounds became a public park a few years later.) Now you are on the south side of the hill and the ground gently slopes away towards the green copper roof of the **Commonwealth Institute** and Kensington High Street beyond. Go straight on out of the park, over Holland Walk and through the bollards into Duchess of Bedford's Walk. Skirting the hill in a slightly downhill direction, cross Campden Hill Road into Holland Street, heading for St Mary Abbots Church ahead. At Hornton Street turn right and walk down the hill past Kensington town hall and library to Kensington High Street and the end of the walk. The Underground station is on the other side of the High Street.

CAMPDEN HILL'S EAST SIDE AND THE OTHER SPURS

To the north and west, as this walk has just shown, the Campden Hill spur comes to a relatively precipitous conclusion. In the east, or in other words towards central London, however, it slopes very gently down to the valley of the Westbourne, dammed in the 18th century to form the Long Water and the Serpentine lake that divides Kensington Gardens and Hyde Park.

The spur on the other side of the Westbourne runs away from the Hampstead region of the Northern Heights along Fitzjohn's Avenue and Finchley Road and then stops short on the north bank of the Serpentine. Its descent from there, through Belgravia to Pimlico, is much more gentle. Cycle from Marble Arch to Victoria, and it's downhill all the way.

The next spur is a dramatic one featuring Primrose Hill, an excellent viewpoint close to central London and therefore to some extent a better one than Parliament Hill despite the fact that it is 100 feet (30 metres) lower. It takes about 10 minutes to walk to Primrose Hill from Chalk Farm Underground Station. Come out of the station on Adelaide Road and cross to Bridge Approach. This leads straight into Regent's Park Road. Follow this road round to the park and turn right into Primrose Hill Road. Go immediately left through the gate and climb straight up to the top of the hill.

Beginning at Hampstead, the Primrose Hill spur runs down to a pronounced saddle where Elsworthy Rise crosses King Henry's Road. The spur is at its narrowest here so several major railway lines – including those from St Pancras and Euston stations – take the opportunity to tunnel through at this point, as a quick glance at a London map will show.

From the saddle (165 feet; 50 metres) the ground rises steeply to Primrose Hill (220 feet; 67 metres) where a panorama board identifies the major landmarks in the City and the West End. In addition, to the left you can clearly see across the valley of the Fleet river to the next spur, with the old Caledonian market clocktower a prominent landmark. To the west, the rather narrower valley contains the Tyburn. Beyond are the chimneys of Battersea Power Station and the distinctive silhouette of Ernö Goldfinger's Trellick Tower. South beyond the West End you can make out the streets on the far side of the river, the Crystal Palace TV mast and, on the horizon, the Surrey hills.

At the foot of the hill, the Regent's Canal cuts across the spur in a slight depression. Between Regent's Park and the river, the ground gently slopes down across Oxford Street to Piccadilly, from where, as we have seen, the descent to the flood plain (i.e. St James's Park and **Buckingham Palace**) is quite steep.

The Islington spur

The fourth and most easterly spur, the Islington spur, is aligned in a more south-easterly direction than its neighbours. Running away from Highgate down Dartmouth Park Road, it forms a saddle in the vicinity of Tufnell Park Underground Station. Here the railway line tunnels through in the Cathcart Hill/Spencer Rise area. The spur then rises again – its crest followed by Brecknock Road – to Caledonian Park (158 feet; 48 metres). Here the old clocktower of the Caledonian market (1855–1939) forms a landmark visible for miles around. Headwaters of the rivers on either side of the spur once again cut back here, creating another narrow saddle or col, and this time it is the east-coast main line from King's Cross that seizes the tunnelling opportunity. By contrast, the Caledonian Road bravely climbs over the top.

The spur turns east here for about half a mile (1 kilometre) and then, in the Barnsbury Street area of Islington, resumes its southerly drift for over a mile (1.6 kilometres), dropping less than 20 feet (6 metres) over the whole of this distance. The drop to the lower terrace begins at Claremont Square on Pentonville Road. This is where we take the second of our spur walks.

THE ISLINGTON SPUR WALK

This circular walk through some of the most elegant but least-known streets and squares in London explores both a prominent snout on the spur and the edge of the 100-foot terrace. It includes a spectacular view of the BT Tower and, at its furthest point, an excellent pub called the Albion.

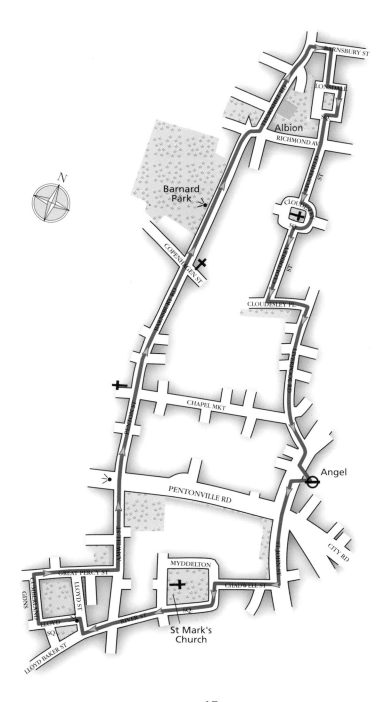

Start/Finish:	Angel Underground (Northern Line).
Length:	2 miles (3 km).
Time:	1½ hours.
Refreshments:	The Albion pub; otherwise all manner of places around Angel Underground Station at the start/finish point.
Sights:	Camden Passage antiques market (Wednesdays and Saturdays) is literally within a stone's throw of Angel Underground Station.
Note:	The views are mainly to the west, so the walk is best done in the morning with the sun behind you.

Turn left out of Angel Underground Station and walk down to the crossroads. Cross to the right and stand on the corner in front of the Cooperative Bank. You are not quite on the snout of the spur here (the ground rises up to it on the right), but looking left you can see the fall-away to the east and ahead down St John Street you can see the ground level beginning to descend to the 50-foot terrace level of the City. On a bicycle you can freewheel from here virtually all the way to Smithfield Market, a distance of almost a mile (1.6 kilometres).

Cross over Pentonville Road and walk down the right-hand side of St John Street. At Chadwell Street turn right. In Myddelton Square, go left round St Mark's Church and continue on into River Street. All the time the ground is steadily sloping downhill to the left.

Spectacular view

From River Street cross Amwell Street into Lloyd Baker Street. When you get to Lloyd Square turn right and then left along the north side of the square. Now you have come round to the west side of the spur and the ground falls sharply away to the Fleet valley, providing a spectacular view of the BT Tower over a mile (1.6 kilometres) away. Walk down the north side of this pretty and little-known square (developed by the Lloyd Baker family in the 1820s and in their possession until as recently as 1975) and, just as you are about to go out of the square, turn right up some steps into Cumberland Gardens. (This, incidentally, must surely be one of the most desirable places in London to live: peaceful location, good views, elegant architecture and all within walking distance of the City.) At the end of the road turn right up

Opposite: Encountering unusual specialist shops like the City Clockshop in Amwell Street is one of the pleasures of walking London's lesser-known streets.

Great Percy Street and then left into Amwell Street and walk up to the junction with Pentonville Road. At this point you are on the snout of the spur and on the edge of the 100-foot terrace. To the left down the hill the spire and roofs of St Pancras Station are the main feature. To the right the embankment in the middle of the square contains a reservoir with a history stretching back well over 300 years. The original reservoir was constructed in the early 1600s to hold water brought from Amwell in Hertfordshire (hence Amwell Street), 20 miles (32 kilometres) away, by means of a special canal constructed by the New River Company (hence River Street). City merchant Sir Hugh Myddelton (hence Myddelton Square) was the head of the company. From the reservoir the water flowed down the hill in pipes to the City. The New River still supplies water to London, but its terminal reservoir is now at Stoke Newington, 3 miles (5 kilometres) north of here.

The last viewpoint

Now cross Pentonville Road into Penton Street and keep walking when Penton Street becomes Barnsbury Road. At this point you are directly above the tunnel that takes the Regent's Canal straight through the Islington spur. You are also walking across the 100-foot terrace and following the eastern edge of the spur. This becomes more clear when, having crossed Copenhagen Street, you arrive at Barnard Park and look out west over the Fleet valley, which is much broader here than it was back at Lloyd Square.

This is the last viewpoint on the walk. Next is the Albion pub. Carry on to the end of Barnsbury Road and then go right and left by a garden into Thornhill Road. The Albion is on the right. To return to Angel Underground Station, carry on along Thornhill Road to Barnsbury Street. Here turn right and then right again into Lonsdale Square, built about 1840 on land belonging to the Drapers' Company (one of the City livery companies – see page 154) in a Gothic style. Go right or left through the square and cross Richmond Avenue into Stonefield Street. This leads to Cloudesley Square, of a more conventional design. Again go right or left through the square and into Cloudesley Street. Then turn left into Cloudesley Place and right into Liverpool Road. Soon you are back at Angel Underground Station.

END OF THE ISLINGTON SPUR

The Islington spur ends in two little 60-foot (18-metre) high hills in the City, Ludgate Hill and Cornhill, divided by a depression. These are the most historic parts of London, for the city's Roman founders planted their most important buildings on the summits: the amphitheatre and fort on Ludgate Hill (today the site of **St Paul's Cathedral**) and the forum and basilica on

Cornhill (today the site of Leadenhall Market). In the olden days, people thought Ludgate Hill was the higher of the two, hence the 300-year-old inscription on a stone on the left-hand side of the entrance to Panyer Alley Steps next to St Paul's Underground Station: 'When ye have sought the City round, yet still this is the highest ground. August 27th, 1688.' In actual fact, Cornhill is about 1 foot (30 centimetres) higher.

The Walbrook river valley

The depression dividing the two hills – obvious, for example, in the way Cannon Street dips between Budge Row and Walbrook – is all that remains of the valley of the Walbrook river. Originally this was quite steep-sided, but as early as the 15th century it was flattened out when the river was covered over. Accumulations since then have further smoothed it over.

Today the Walbrook, known to sewer engineers as the London Bridge Sewer, runs 30–35 feet (9–10 metres) below ground level and meets the Thames about 120 feet (35 metres) west of Cannon Street Station. Its route is marked by All Hallows London Wall Church (the river entered the City through a culvert in the wall just to the west of the church), St Margaret Lothbury Church (built on vaults over the river), the exposed foundations of the Roman Temple of Mithras in Queen Victoria Street (the temple stood on the river's western bank), the aforementioned dip in Cannon Street (although the lowest point in this dip seems to be at Walbrook, the river's course is actually about 150 feet (45 metres) west and a monument in Cloak Lane marking the site of the church of St John the Baptist upon Walbrook (the river flowed past the west wall of the church, destroyed in the Great Fire). If you look at a map of the City's wards, you will find that the western boundaries of Walbrook and Dowgate wards correspond exactly to the river's course.

THE LOST RIVERS OF LONDON

With the exception of the Lee, all of the other central London tributaries of the Thames on the north side of the river have gone the same way as the Walbrook; in other words they have been covered over or piped in and turned into storm sewers whose main function is to carry away rainwater from roadside gutters. Despite the fact that they have been buried, however, many clues to their existence remain visible on the surface.

We will now set out on foot to discover some of them. The three following routes trace the lower, most interesting reaches of central London's most significant 'lost' rivers: the Westbourne, the Tyburn and the Fleet. In general, these walks reveal a secret London of winding lanes, narrow back streets and picturesque mews to which few people go.

THE WESTBOURNE RIVER WALK

The Westbourne (meaning West Stream) begins as several streamlets flowing down the hill to the west of Hampstead. One of these streamlets can apparently be seen beneath a manhole at the west end of Alexandra Road in NW8. The major streamlets flow together to form the main river in the region of Kilburn High Road Station. In the 18th century a spring on the bank of the river here (commemorated today in Springfield Lane and Spring Walk) was developed into a popular spa called Kilburn Wells. A stone plaque at first-floor level at the corner of Kilburn High Road and Belsize Road marks the spa's site. From Belsize Road the river flows through Maida Vale and Carlton Vale and then, having picked up a tributary from Kensal Rise turns east along Shirland Road. At the end of Shirland Road it veers south under the Regent's Canal and the humpy Westbourne Green. From here it flows down Gloucester Mews West and Upbrook Mews to Brook Mews North just outside Hyde Park, where we join it. First, however, we have to make our way to Brook Mews from Paddington Underground Station.

Start:	Paddington Underground Station (District, Circle, Hammersmith & City and Bakerloo Lines).
Finish:	Sloane Square Underground Station (District and Circle Lines).
Length:	3 miles (5 km).
Time:	2½ hours.
Refreshments:	Around the half-way stage a choice of either the Dell café/restaurant in Hyde Park next to the Serpentine or, just a little bit further on, one of the cosy pubs in picturesque Kinnerton Street. Otherwise, Paddington Underground near the beginning of the walk and Sloane Square Underground towards the end are both surrounded by all kinds of eating places.
Sights:	Hyde Park, the Serpentine, Knightsbridge, Belgravia, Sloane Square, **Chelsea Hospital**.
Note:	If possible, plan to finish the walk at low or lowish tide on the Thames; otherwise it may not be possible to see the Westbourne's outfall. To find out when low tide is, either consult the current edition of *Whitaker's Almanack* in your local library or ring the Port of London harbourmaster on 020 7265 2656.

Come out of Paddington Underground Station opposite the Hilton London Paddington Hotel and turn left. Cross Spring Street and carry on down the hill, passing the entrance to Conduit Mews on the left. Spring Street and Conduit Mews (and nearby Conduit Place, which you don't see) commemorate a local spring that was used to supply the City of London with water from 1471 until 1812. This was the main spring in the area and its name, Bayard's Watering, became in a slightly altered fashion that of the whole district: Bayswater.

Brooks and mews

Cross Westbourne Terrace and go past the entrance (on the left) to Smallbrook Mews, probably taking its name from a little tributary of the Westbourne. Cross Gloucester Terrace. When you get to the next mews entrances – Upbrook Mews on the right and Brook Mews North on the left – you are on the actual course of the Westbourne, which flows from right to left. Turn left into Brook Mews North and walk down to the far end. If the gate on the left is open, go through it, turn right and make your way to the far right-hand corner of the garden. Here turn left into Elms Mews. If the gate is closed, follow the road round to the right, turn left into Craven Terrace and then, when Craven Terrace bends right, branch left down some steps (i.e. down the river bank) into Elms Mews. Elms Mews brings you out on to the Bayswater Road at a definite low point. When this was still open country there was a bridge here, with a coaching inn called the Swan next to it. The bridge has gone, but look to your right and you will see that the Swan, opened in 1775, is still very much in existence.

Hyde Park

Turn left on Bayswater Road, cross at the lights to the other side and go through Marlborough Gate into Hyde Park. Ahead of you now is a long stretch of water: first, four fountains and then the Long Water, the latter created in the 1730s by the simple expedient of damming up the Westbourne. In the foreground is the ornate fountain pump house and, just in front of that, the Westbourne's original outfall into the Long Water with the tops of its three brick-lined arches poking up through the grass. Today the Westbourne flows not into the Long Water (which is filled by rainwater run-off from the surrounding slopes) but into the Ranelagh Sewer, a Victorian conduit constructed beneath the lake's left bank.

Go to the left of the pump house and walk along beside the fountains and then the lake. As you do so, you are contouring round the end of the spur running down from the Northern Heights described earlier. After a while you come to a fork. Keep right here to stay close to the water and walk

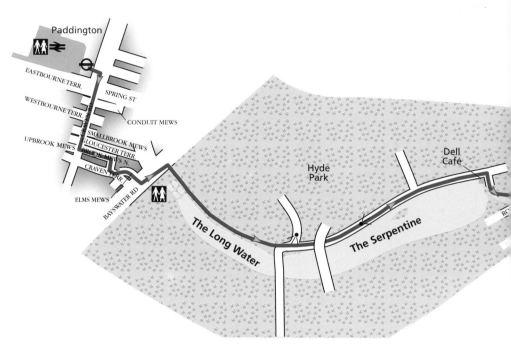

underneath the bridge. On the other side (where the lake is known as the Serpentine) you can see to the right the tower of Knightsbridge cavalry barracks. Later another tower comes into view in the far distance: the Victoria Tower of the Palace of Westminster.

The Dell

Carry on to the end of the lake and the dam. After the Dell café, turn right down into the Dell. On the way you pass, on the right, an inscription commemorating another ancient water supply, this time for Westminster. This supply was started before the Norman Conquest (1066) and was not cut off until 1861. The Dell is a pretty little water garden formed beneath the Serpentine's dam. The overflow flows into the buried Westbourne (i.e. the Ranelagh Sewer) if the Serpentine is full. If the Serpentine is not getting enough run-off from its catchment area, it is recycled back into the lake.

Carry straight on from the Dell, crossing a tarmac cycle track, the Rotten Row riding track and South Carriage Drive. Beneath this road is a huge brick-lined cavern where the Westbourne is joined by the overflow from the Serpentine and by a little tributary called the Tyburn Brook (not to be confused with the Tyburn), which runs down from the Marble Arch area.

Knightsbridge

Having crossed South Carriage Drive, go through Albert Gate to come into Knightsbridge. As the second part of the name suggests, there was indeed a bridge here once carrying the main road – since ancient times an important highway to the west – over the Westbourne. Where 'knight' comes from, however, is not as obvious as it seems; it is probably a corruption of a quite different word such as Neyt, the name of the adjoining manor.

From this point – the junction of Albert Gate and Knightsbridge – the Westbourne continues its southerly course across the Thames flood plain.

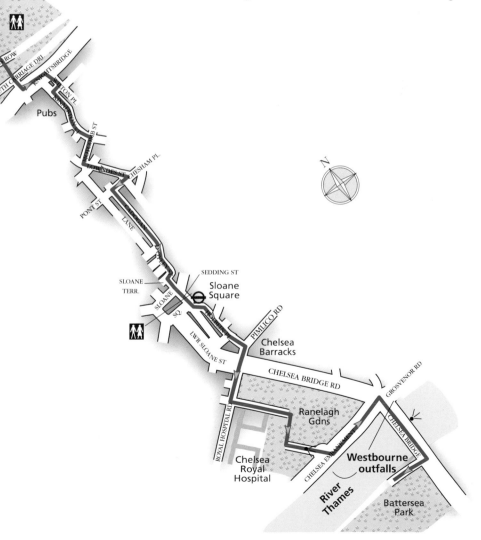

Being so flat, the plain reveals few signs of the river's course, but there are one or two clues, for example in the layout of certain streets, which help to keep us on the right track. To find the first of these clues, we have to make a short detour to the east of the river.

The east bank
Cross Knightsbridge at the lights and turn left. Take the first right into Wilton Place and then go right again into Kinnerton Street and turn left. Off to the right there are lots of little dead-end mews running off the street at right angles. Altogether there are eight of these little enclaves, all belonging to the Duke of Westminster's Grosvenor estate (notice the estate signs and the wheatsheaf plaque fixed to the fronts of some of the houses – more details on page 67). Today they provide bijou residences for the wealthy, but originally they were yards and workshops used by the tradesmen serving the grand houses on the duke's newly built Belgravia estate. The river ran along their far end (no doubt making a convenient lavatory and rubbish tip), which is why they are all blocked off.

At the end of Kinnerton Street, turn right into Motcomb Street. The impressive façade of the Pantechnicon (a supposedly fire-proof warehouse burnt down in 1874) stands on the right just about directly over the river's course. Carry on to the end of the street. The river crosses from left to right in the vicinity of Zafferano's restaurant at No. 15. Now turn left into Lowndes Street. When you get to the traffic lights in Chesham Place, turn right into Pont Street, so named because of another bridge over the Westbourne here. The French word was probably chosen in order to make the new development (dating from the 1830s) sound more chic.

Pont Street to Sloane Square
The bridge, marked on maps up to the 1820s at least, seems to have been where Cadogan Lane now is, so turn left into the lane when you come to it and walk down to the end where it becomes D'Oyley Street. Follow D'Oyley Street round into Sloane Terrace and take the first left into Sedding Street. A zebra crossing at the end brings you into Sloane Square.

Sloane Square Underground Station ahead provides a good opportunity to get a new fix on the exact course of the Westbourne, for the river is carried over the tracks in a huge iron pipe clearly visible from the platforms. You can try to persuade the staff to let you down free to have a quick look, but they will probably make you buy a ticket first. From the station, the river carries

Opposite: The Italian Water Garden in Hyde Park, complete with arcaded Italianate summer house and fountains, was created in 1861.

on down Holbein Place, first left out of the station. At the end of Holbein Place it splits up into several different channels to form a kind of delta. The main channel carries straight on under Chelsea Barracks and cuts across Chelsea Bridge Road and the grounds of **Chelsea Hospital** before flowing out into the Thames through an arched tunnel in the embankment wall.

The Chelsea Hospital channel

The barracks are inaccessible for obvious reasons, so we cannot follow this route directly. We can go through the grounds of Chelsea Hospital (the home for old soldiers, founded in 1682), however, and pick up the river again before its confluence with the Thames. From Holbein Place, turn right into Pimlico Road. Cross Chelsea Bridge Road at the lights and walk along Royal Hospital Road to the hospital's entrance on the left. Turn in here and walk down the road and through the big gates leading to the tree-lined avenue. The river cuts across Ranelagh Gardens – from which the Ranelagh Sewer gets its name – on the left, crosses the avenue and meets the Thames almost directly ahead. Go down the little slope in the avenue and turn right by the tennis courts. Then go left down the central path leading past the 1849 Chilianwallah memorial towards the gutted but still majestic Battersea Power Station on the far side of the river. (Chilianwallah, incidentally, was the British Army's costliest battle in the conquest of India.)

Go through the gates at the far end and cross Chelsea Embankment using the traffic island on the left. Where the pavement meets the wall you will see the date 1858 carved into one of the granite blocks. What this refers to is not known (it can't be the building of the embankment because that was 15 years later), but it serves as a useful pointer to the mouth of the Westbourne, for if you look over the wall you will see it directly below. For the intrepid who want to get a closer look, there are some stairs about 100 yards to the right. Otherwise you can get a good view from Battersea Park opposite.

Other channels

When you come back from the park, cross the bridge on the downstream (i.e. power station) side. From here you will see two more tunnel entrances and the entrance to a large dock in between the road bridge and the railway bridge. These are the ends of the delta channels mentioned earlier.

The dock is all that remains of an extensive canal and reservoir system begun by the Chelsea Waterworks Company in 1725 to supply drinking water to Mayfair. A century later it was extended by the Grosvenor family, hence its present name, the Grosvenor Canal. Until the mid-1990s Westminster City Council used it for barging away rubbish to tips in the Thames estuary. Now it is being regenerated with houses, shops and offices surrounding a marina. For a closer view of the dock, stand on Grosvenor Road where it crosses the dock entrance and look over the railings.

To return to Sloane Square Underground Station and the end of the walk, follow Chelsea Bridge Road and its continuation, Lower Sloane Street, straight up to Sloane Square.

THE TYBURN RIVER WALK

The Tyburn (meaning Boundary Stream) rises on Haverstock Hill near Hampstead, in the vicinity of Shepherd's Walk and its junction with Fitzjohn's Avenue. (A plaque indicates the approximate position of Shepherd's Well – the original, but now lost, source of the Tyburn.) Flowing down through Swiss Cottage, it is then said to cross the Regent's Canal and enter Regent's Park by means of an aqueduct incorporated into pedestrian-only Charlbert Bridge. The park manager, however, says this is not the case. He also says that the Tyburn does not supply Regent's Park lake, although other authorities claim that it does. Whatever the truth on these points, the Tyburn certainly begins its journey through the West End in the Baker Street area, where we join it.

Start:	Baker Street Underground (Jubilee, Metropolitan, Bakerloo, Hammersmith & City and Circle Lines).
Finish:	Pimlico or Vauxhall Bridge Underground (both Victoria Line).
Length:	3½ miles (5.5 km).
Time:	2½ hours.
Refreshments:	There are plenty of pubs, restaurants, wine bars and sandwich bars along the length of this walk, except for the last half mile (kilometre). Shepherd Market in Mayfair, one of London's most attractive little enclaves, is perhaps the best refreshment stop: it's about half-way and it has a good selection of places to eat and drink.
Sights:	Oxford Street, Mayfair, Green Park, **Buckingham Palace** and the **Queen's Gallery**.
Note:	If possible, plan to finish the walk at low or lowish tide on the Thames; otherwise it may not be possible to see the Tyburn's outfall. To find out when low tide is, consult the current edition of *Whitaker's Almanack* or ring the Port of London harbourmaster on 020 7265 2656.

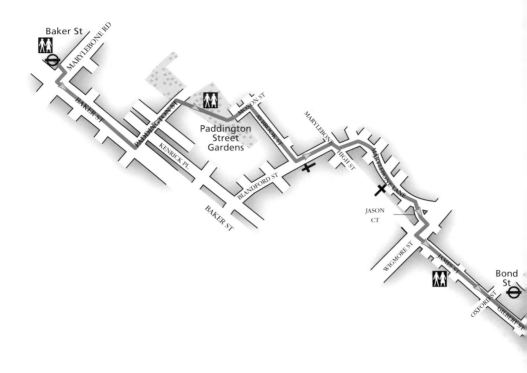

Come out of Baker Street Underground Station on the south side of Marylebone Road and walk down the left-hand side of Baker Street, heading in the same direction as the traffic. At the second left, which is Paddington Street, turn left. The river actually continues south for a little way almost as far as Blandford Street before it also turns left, but because of the unhelpful street layout we have to make our turn here. If you look down Kenrick Place on the right it is possible to see the low point where the river runs across just before Blandford Street.

Carry on along Paddington Street until you reach Paddington Street Gardens. Turn right into the gardens and make your way diagonally across to the far left-hand corner. Go through the gates out of the park into Moxon Street and turn right into Aybrook Street (the river was sometimes known as the Aye Brook as well as the Tyburn). At the bottom of the street, where we pick up the river again, turn left into Blandford Street.

Marylebone

When you get to Marylebone High Street, cross over to the Angel in the Fields pub and continue along Marylebone Lane. The High Street was the centre of the old village of Marylebone, its name derived, via St Mary-le-bourne, from Tyburn. The lane was the road connecting the village with London. At this point the lane stuck to the riverside, hence its winding course. Elsewhere in this part of London the streets are laid out on a more or less regular grid.

Stay with Marylebone Lane until you come to a fork with a shop called The Button Queen at its dividing point. Here the lane goes off to the left away from the river; we go right into Jason Court. At Wigmore Street turn right and then, crossing over at the lights, left into James Street. Walk down this street to its junction with Oxford Street. Here, look left and right and you will see that you are definitely in the river valley. In 1941 the river was seen flowing through the bottom of a bomb crater here.

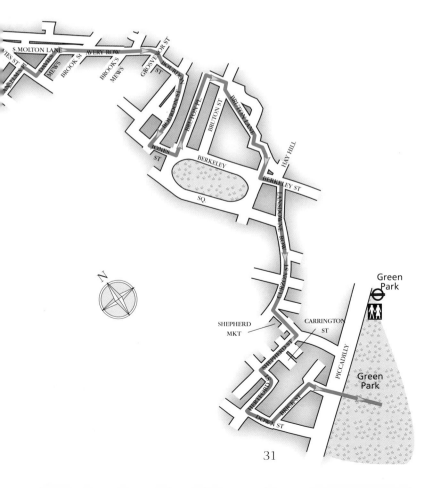

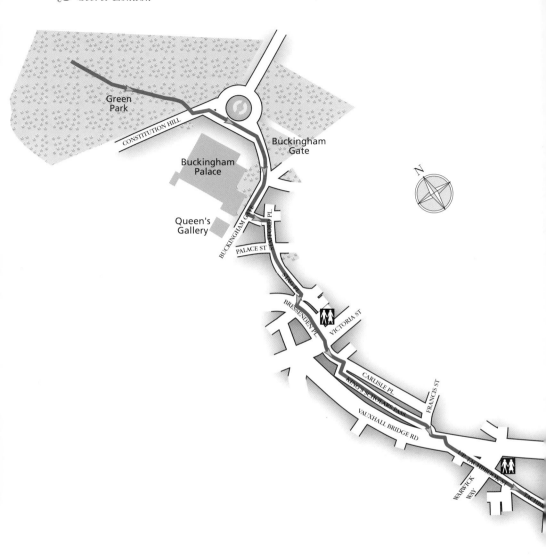

Mayfair

Carry on now into Gilbert Street and so into the exclusive residential district of Mayfair. Somewhere here the river bends east again, but the street levels have been so much altered that it is impossible to pinpoint the exact course. However, the steep drop into St Anselm's Place is at least a clue. Turn left here, right at the end into Davies Street and then immediately left into Davies Mews. At the end of the mews, turn right into

South Molton Lane, cross Brook Street (note the watery name) and enter narrow Avery Row, built in the 1720s over the newly culverted Tyburn by bricklayer Henry Avery. The low point in the middle is the real ground level, and the west side of the valley can be seen stretching up Brook's Mews to your right. Behind and in front of you, Brook Street and Grosvenor Street respectively have been raised up on artificial embankments. It's these embankments, or causeways, that create the constant ups and downs as we walk along what should be a flat river bed.

Now climb up to Grosvenor Street, cross, and go through the opening into Bourdon Street. Again, there is a marked descent to the valley bottom. As buildings now block our path, we have a short detour. Turn right up the hill (keeping left when the road forks) and then left near the top into pedestrian-only Jones Street. This brings you out into Berkeley Square. From the corner on the left, you can see the bottom of the valley at the far end of the square and the bank on the far side rising up to Piccadilly. We shall come to this point shortly, but first we return to where we left the river in Bourdon Street. Turn left into Bruton Place and go down to the bottom, past the Guinea pub. Here, follow the road round to the right, cross Bruton Street and then continue along Bruton Lane, keeping the Coach and Horses pub on the left. When Bruton Lane bends to the right, look up and left to see the19th-century stone plaque on the wall, marking the boundary between the Berkeley estate and the City's (Conduit Mead) estate (see page 57). Before these streets were built, the Tyburn river was the boundary between the two properties.

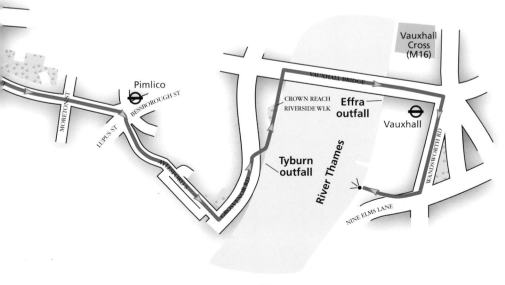

Near the end of Bruton Lane, a gated private road follows the course of the river. Bear right here and then turn left into Berkeley Street. Hay Hill and the rising ground up to Piccadilly bar the river's southerly progress towards the Thames and force it to pursue a more westerly course. We follow it by crossing Berkeley Street into pedestrian-only Lansdowne Row. This little street of small shops and sandwich bars was created by paving over the river when it formed a boundary between the grounds of two former aristocratic town houses: Devonshire House and Lansdowne House.

Shepherd Market

From Lansdowne Row, continue into Curzon Street. Just beyond the Third Church of Christ Scientist on the right, turn left through the opening at No. 47, into Shepherd Market. Go down to the King's Arms pub and turn right. The original market from which this little enclave of narrow streets, pubs and restaurants takes its name must have grown up on the river bank, for after flowing west to avoid Hay Hill the Tyburn continues its southerly course here, possibly through Carrington Street (second on your left), Yarmouth Place and the bottom of Brick Street. Carrington Street (significantly) is a dead end, so we must take a detour to get to Yarmouth Place and Brick Street.

Carry on a little way and turn left into Hertford Street. Follow the road round to the right and take the first left into Down Street. (Ahead on the right is the entrance to the disused Down Street Underground Station – see page 48.) Turn left again into Brick Street. Yarmouth Place is at the bottom of the hill on the left. Follow Brick Street, which used to be called Engine Street ('engine' referring to a mill or other machine powered by the river), round to the right and you come out on Piccadilly. That you are back on the actual course of the river is confirmed by the way the ground rises to both your left and your right.

Green Park

Cross Piccadilly and go through the gate into Green Park. You can now see the gently sloping valley, shorn of buildings, curving gently to the right and then, near the bottom, nudged by Constitution Hill protruding from the right, equally gently to the left. Here, in very ancient times, the open Tyburn disappeared into the marshy ground of the Thames flood plain, as described above. Later it was used to fill the lake in St James's Park (a function fulfilled today by artesian wells). Now, safely contained in its brick-lined tunnel, it continues on its way beneath **Buckingham Palace** to its meeting point with the Thames, about $1\frac{1}{3}$ miles (2 kilometres) away.

Opposite: Green Park, once watered by the burbling Tyburn brook, is a good place to stop as you follow the now lost river's route from Baker Street.

To the Thames

It has to be admitted that the walk from here to the Thames, which takes about 50 minutes and is along flat ground, is not quite as interesting or varied as the stretch from Marylebone to Green Park, but it is well worth doing nonetheless. The reward at the end is to see where the Tyburn flows out into the Thames.

To begin, cross Constitution Hill at the lights, pass in front of Buckingham Palace and keep following the railings round to the right. After passing through Buckingham Gate, cross the main road (also called Buckingham Gate) and turn right. Turn left at No. 4 Buckingham Gate (opposite the entrance to the **Queen's Gallery**) and walk through the pedestrian-only opening into Stafford Place. Turn right here, cross Palace Street and continue into Stag Place. At the far end, go through the colourful sculpture and then straight on into Bressenden Place. At the lights, cross straight over Victoria Street to Carlisle Place and take the first right into King's Scholars' Passage. (If the gates are closed, carry on along Carlisle Place and turn right on Francis Street.) The passage is a rather smelly service road between the backs of tall buildings. Its curious name comes from King's Scholars' Pond, into which the Tyburn flowed somewhere near here when the area was still open countryside. The King's Scholars themselves were schoolboys at nearby Westminster School (see page 104). When the Tyburn was covered over, this section was christened the King's Scholars' Pond Sewer.

At the end of the passage, cross busy Vauxhall Bridge Road diagonally into Upper Tachbrook Street. You could be forgiven for thinking that Tachbrook is in some way a reference to the Tyburn. In fact it is a place in Warwickshire, which in the 18th century was owned by a man who also owned land here. (The man, incidentally, was royal gardener Henry Wise.)

Carry on along Tachbrook Street, crossing Warwick Way, Charlwood Street and Moreton Street on the way. At the end, the river carries straight on across the main road (Lupus/Bessborough Street), but we have to deviate slightly and bear right along Aylesford Street. At the end of the street, cross Grosvenor Road and turn left back towards the river's course, passing the Thames-side Chester Wharf.

The Tyburn outflow

When you reach Tyburn House and Rio Cottage, you are back with the river once more. This, moreover, is the precise point where it finally flows into the Thames. Beneath the houses there is a semicircular opening in the river wall about 10 feet (3 metres) high and 15 feet (4.5 metres) across. Set back about 20 feet (6 metres) inside it is a heavy iron sluice gate installed, as the plaque on Rio Cottage says, in 1832. If you go round the corner into Crown

Reach Riverside Walk and look over the parapet, you can see the river's outflow channel.

You used to be able to get a close-up view of the brick-lined tunnel and sluice gate by climbing down the ladder on to the mud flats, but it is now blocked. Another way is to go to the public garden on the opposite bank. To reach it, walk along the riverside to Vauxhall Bridge, cross, turn right into Wandsworth Road and right again into Nine Elms Lane and keep going until you come to the garden. Provided you cross the bridge on the right-hand (upstream) side you will also see – at the point where the bridge meets the bank – the sluice gate of the Effra, one of the main 'lost rivers' of the south side of the Thames. There is a similar gate on the other side of the bridge (under the headquarters of MI6, Britain's Secret Service – see page 118) which is labelled 'Effra', but this is actually only a storm sewer.

Locations of both Pimlico and Vauxhall Underground stations, at either of which the walk can end, are shown on the map.

THE FLEET RIVER WALK

The highly conspicuous sources of the Fleet (Anglo-Saxon for tidal inlet) are the large bathing ponds on the Hampstead and Highgate sides of Hampstead Heath and the lake in the grounds of Kenwood. The Hampstead source flows down Fleet Road and is joined by the Highgate source just before passing under Kentish Town Road near its junction with Hawley Road. Having flowed under the Regent's Canal in the Lyme Street area, it links up with St Pancras Way at the latter's junction with Pratt Street. St Pancras Way is an old road, and the Fleet once flowed beside it just as the Tyburn flowed beside Marylebone Lane. Passing Old St Pancras Church, the river then flows between St Pancras Station and King's Cross Station, where we join it.

Start:	King's Cross Station (Circle, Victoria, Northern, Piccadilly, Hammersmith & City and Metropolitan Lines and trains.)
Finish:	Blackfriars Station (District and Circle Lines and trains).
Length:	2 miles (3.2 km).
Time:	1½ hours.
Refreshments:	There are pubs, sandwich bars and restaurants all along the route, but Clerkenwell Green is the best place to stop. It has a variety of eating and drinking places (many with outdoor seating), is exactly half-way and has a villagey atmosphere.

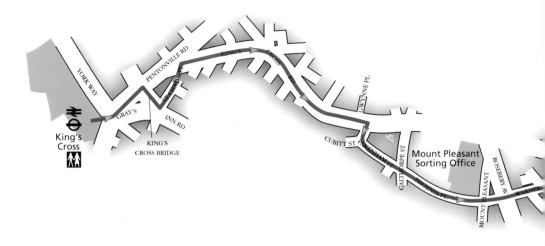

Sights: **Mount Pleasant Sorting Office**, the Clerks'
Well, Clerkenwell Green, Smithfield Market,
St Paul's Cathedral, Fleet Street, Bridewell.

Note: If possible plan to finish the walk at low or
lowish tide on the Thames; otherwise it may
not be possible to see the Fleet's outfall. To find
out when low tide is, either consult the current
edition of *Whitaker's Almanack* in your local
library or ring the Port of London
harbourmaster on 020 7265 2656.

On the forecourt of King's Cross Station facing away from the entrance, turn
left. Cross York Way into Pentonville Road and walk along to the traffic
lights. Ahead, Pentonville Road climbs the steep hill forming both the west
side of the Barnsbury spur, running down from the Northern Heights, and
the east side of the Fleet valley.

Cross right into King's Cross Bridge, a short road covering the railway and
Underground lines beneath. As you will see at various points along the
course of the walk, both these lines run through a deep cutting – sometimes
open, sometimes covered – as far as Farringdon Station, where they divide.
The railway line, continuing on through City Thameslink Station and
crossing the river at Blackfriars, is one of only two lines in central London
to run right through the city. Significantly, both use river valleys to do so.

This one, the Thameslink Line, obviously uses the valley of the Fleet. The other one, the West London Line passing the Olympia and Earl's Court exhibition centres, follows the course of Counter's Creek.

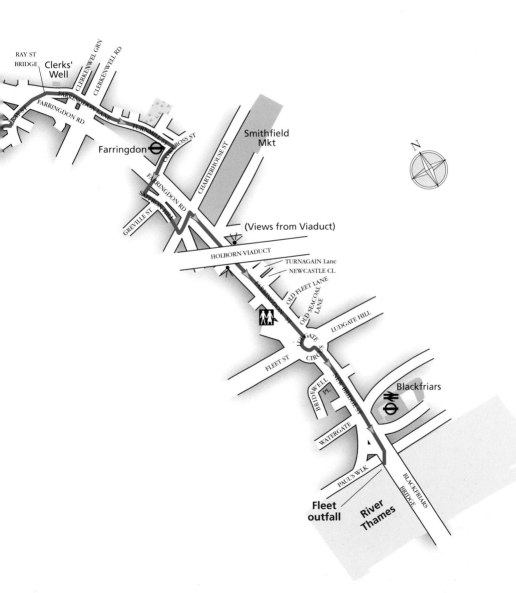

St Chad's spa

From King's Cross Bridge, take the first left into St Chad's Place and walk down the hill. Standing at the low point, you can see over the wall into King's Cross Thameslink Station in the cutting below. The building of the Underground line through this district in the 1860s destroyed the last remaining part of St Chad's Gardens, a pleasure ground surrounding a once popular medicinal well, which in the 18th century attracted up to a thousand people a week to drink its waters. Later in the walk we come to the site of another Fleet-side spa that was an even bigger draw than this.

St Chad's Place now narrows into a passage and, bending left, brings you out on King's Cross Road. Turn right and follow the road as it bends round to the right. On the left the roads all climb up the east side of the Fleet valley and several (Weston Rise, for example) feature the tell-tale word 'Rise' in their names. Beyond the former magistrates' court and police station, the road changes direction and swings round to the left, keeping close to the river's meandering course.

Bagnigge Wells

Just beyond the garage on the right there is a terrace of houses, all with balconies at first-floor level. Here stood Bagnigge Wells, the other famous spa mentioned earlier and one of the best-attended of all the spas surrounding London during the spa-crazy 18th century. The Fleet itself flowed through the spa gardens, and there were seats on the bank 'for such as chuse to smoke or drink cyder, ale etc. which are not permitted in other parts of the garden'. Today the only relic of the spa (besides the name of nearby Wells Square) is the inscribed stone set into the front wall of the first house in the terrace, thought to mark the north-western boundary of the gardens. The stone is dated 1680, which is particularly interesting because this is about the time when Bagnigge House was used as a summer retreat by Charles II's mistress, Nell Gwynn. Nell's association with the area is commemorated in Gwynne [sic] Place on the opposite side of the road. The 'Pinder a Wakefeilde' mentioned on the plaque refers to a famous old pub called the Pindar of Wakefield on nearby Gray's Inn Road. It survived until just a few years ago when it was taken over and renamed The Water Rats. The original Pindar opened in 1517.

Mount Pleasant

Beyond the terrace turn right into Cubitt Street and then first left into Pakenham Street. The river swings right here towards Pakenham Street to avoid a knob of high ground ahead called Mount Pleasant. As you rise up towards the junction with Calthorpe Street, the knob comes into view with a huge **Royal Mail sorting office** on top. Go straight on into Phoenix Place and down the hill, probably an artificial one intended to graduate the incline of Calthorpe Street up the west side of the Fleet valley. When you get to the road called Mount Pleasant, the true valley bottom reappears to the right. Carry straight on here into Warner Street and go under the bridge carrying Rosebery Avenue across the valley. The river now cuts into the bank on the right, up which climb several streets with 'hill' in their names, for example Eyre Street Hill and Back Hill. The top of the hill was once a large garden attached to the Bishop of Ely's London house, hence other local horticulturally flavoured street names such as Vine Hill and Herbal Hill.

Clerkenwell

At the end of Warner Street, turn left into Ray Street, its sides framing the spire of Clerkenwell parish church ahead. Cross Farringdon Road and follow Ray Street Bridge round to the right towards the City Pride pub. Clerkenwell's name comes from the Clerks' Well, a spring of pure water on the east bank of the Fleet, which in the Middle Ages was associated with the Company of Parish Clerks in the City. Having been lost for centuries, the old well was rediscovered in 1924 and is now visible through a window in No. 16 Farringdon Lane (Well Court) just beyond the City Pride. The display beside the well includes an exhibition with writing big enough to read from outside and, on the left wall, an enlarged reproduction of a 16th-century map that clearly shows Clerkenwell and the broad River Fleet flowing down beside it towards the Thames. From the well, carry on along Farringdon Lane and past the entrance to Clerkenwell Green. Cross Clerkenwell Road and continue into Turnmill Street, so named because of three water mills worked here by the Fleet in the Middle Ages. At the end of the street, turn right by Farringdon Station into Cowcross Street, cross Farringdon Road into Greville Street and turn left into Saffron Hill. This is a reminder that the Bishops of Ely grew a rich crop of saffron crocuses in their hilltop garden here, saffron being widely used in the Middle Ages to mask the taste of rancid meat. Saffron Hill slopes quite steeply down to what is probably something like real street level. At the end you have to climb up some steps to regain the artificially elevated street. The difference between the two must be all of 20 feet (6 metres). From the top of the steps turn left. Ahead on the other side of the valley is Smithfield Market. When this ancient market dealt in live meat, it was the cause of many of the Fleet's problems, for the river was used to wash away the blood and entrails of butchered animals. The resulting pollution can all too easily be imagined.

Holborn Viaduct

At the crossroads, turn right into Farringdon Street and walk down to Holborn Viaduct. Climb the stairs on the right past the huge illustration of the Fleet Valley clearances of the mid 19th century. From the viaduct itself there are fine views of the valley to both north and south. To the north, Farringdon Road was constructed over the Fleet in the 1840s, erasing some of London's most infamous slums at the same time. To the south, the river had been covered over as early as the 1730s and the Fleet Market – two rows of one-storey shops connected by a covered walkway – built on top. By the early 19th century, however, the market had become so badly dilapidated and such a nuisance that it was cleared away and replaced by Farringdon Street.

Holborn Viaduct itself was built in 1869. Connecting Holborn with Newgate Street, the new bridge put an end to the difficult and sometimes dangerous ascents and descents of the steep sides of the Fleet valley, making it much easier for horse-drawn traffic to pass to and fro between the City and the West End.

Descend from the viaduct via the south-east steps and continue along the left side of Farringdon Street. The names of several streets on the left provide more clues to the presence of the 'lost' river. Turnagain Lane was a cul-de-sac ending at the riverside: when you reached it you had to 'turn again' and go back the way you came. When Londoners cooked their food and heated their homes with open fires, much of their coal came by sea from the Newcastle area. Newcastle Close, therefore, may allude to the coal brought up the Fleet by barge, though this is not certain. Old Fleet Lane is obvious. Old Seacoal Lane is definitely a reference to coal traffic on the Fleet. The river was navigable as far as Old Seacoal Lane until 1765 when New Bridge Street, the next and final section of the walk, was built over it.

New Bridge Street and Bridewell

New Bridge Street begins at Ludgate Circus, the meeting point of two ancient thoroughfares: Fleet Street and Ludgate Hill. Here the river slices its way through the 50-foot terrace described earlier. As you make your way down the street, you can see how the ground continues to rise steeply on either side until quite near the Thames.

For 300 years the wide mouth of the Fleet was dominated by a royal palace-turned-prison called Bridewell (another watery name). Although the main part of the Tudor building was pulled down in the 1860s, a reminder of it exists in the name of Bridewell Place on the right. Also, a little further on, the prison's 1805 gatehouse, complete with black spiked gate, still stands. A little further on still is a street with the resonant name of 'Watergate'. This marks the position of the prison's river entrance. It is some distance from the modern Thames ahead, showing how much land has been reclaimed over the past couple of centuries, particularly at this point.

The Fleet outflow

Near the entrance to Watergate you will see an entrance to the Blackfriars subway. Go down here for the final stage of the walk: the search for the point at which the Fleet finally flows out into the Thames after its 4½-mile (7-kilometre) journey from Hampstead Heath. At the foot of the stairs go left and then right, making for exit 5 on the subway map. When you come out into the open air again, don't go up the steps on to the bridge, but instead turn right down to Paul's Walk. At the foot of the steps, lean out over the water and crane your head to the left: if it's low tide you should be rewarded with your Holy Grail – a clear, if oblique, view of the arched entrance to the Fleet tunnel. There is a better view of the entrance from the high-level platform of Blackfriars railway (as opposed to underground) station to your left. This runs out over the river, allowing you to look back and down at the river gate. However, you may need a ticket in order to get onto the platform in the first place.

The walk ends at Blackfriars Station, which is accessible through the subway.

SOUTH OF THE THAMES

Corresponding with the seven Thames tributaries on the north side of the river are seven more on the south side. Starting in the west, these are (with places of confluence with the Thames): Beverley Brook (Putney), the Wandle (Wandsworth), Falcon Brook (Battersea), the Effra (Vauxhall), the Neckinger (Bermondsey), the Earl's Sluice (Rotherhithe) and the Ravensbourne (Deptford). However, the terrain on the south side is not as interesting as it is on the north side (either to describe or to explore), and the south-side rivers are more suburban than the north-side ones. Also, the south-side rivers are less 'secret'. No fewer than three of the seven – Beverley Brook, the Wandle and the Ravensbourne – flow on the surface; a fourth, the Effra, appears in the grounds of a publicly owned country house called Belair in Gallery Road, Dulwich. The mouth of a fifth – the Neckinger – can be seen at St Saviour's Dock next to the Design Museum on Butler's Wharf.

THE SUBTERRANEAN CITY

There is a lot more to London than meets the eye. The hidden parts are not just behind walls; they are also beneath the surface. People have been tunnelling through the London clay for well over a century and a half now, and the result is an extraordinary honeycomb of structures extending up to 200 feet (60 metres) deep below the city streets. Generally, the only signs on the surface are grilles, vents and manhole covers. Of course, much of this subterranean world is familiar to millions of people through the Underground system and the various road and foot tunnels under the Thames. But equally much is not, as we shall see.

UNDERGROUND CITADELS

Probably the most interesting individual complex is the government's system of offices and tunnels under Whitehall. At its heart is a huge subterranean office block beneath the Treasury at the junction of Horse Guards Road, Storey's Gate and Great George Street. Secretly converted within the existing building by filling in the ground floor above with 17 feet (5 metres) of concrete to form a protective shield, it was built in the 1930s and used during the Second World War by Prime Minister Winston Churchill and his War Cabinet. Today most of its 200-odd rooms continue to function as office space, although the most historic parts – the rooms used by Churchill and the cabinet – have been opened to the public as the **Cabinet War Rooms** museum. If you should visit this evocative relic of Britain's darkest hour, remember that what you see is only a relatively small part of a much bigger complex extending over 6 acres (2.5 hectares) around you. The Army engineer responsible for building the War Rooms (Brigadier James Orr) died only in 1993. He received an OBE for his work, but the whole project was so secret that he was never given a citation.

Extending north and south from the War Rooms are two tunnels. The southerly one goes as far as former government offices in Marsham Street. Built during the last war to connect the War Rooms with the government's Rotunda citadel constructed within the old Horseferry Road gasometers, the tunnel (rumoured to emerge in the basement of Westminster Hospital) is now believed to be disused. The partly ivy-clad Rotunda was visible from Marsham Street and Monck Street until 2000, but has since been demolished. The northern tunnel, which is the oldest part of the government system, connects the War Rooms via the 'Q' Whitehall exchange with the government telephone exchange in Craig's Court and Northumberland Avenue, near Charing Cross Station.

It is believed (the government system is very secret) that several branch tunnels lead off this telephone-exchange tunnel. One goes east to the pre-Second World War Army citadel under the Ministry of Defence. (At the end of 1993 news broke that this citadel had just been converted into a brand-new, state-of-the-art headquarters to replace the old Cabinet War Rooms.) Another branch tunnel goes west to the Admiralty citadel, the above-ground section of which forms the ivy-covered concrete blockhouse at the junction of Horse Guards Road and the Mall. A third tunnel burrows its way in the Pall Mall direction and apparently has an exit at the Duke of York's Steps, where there is a door with a doorbell next to it. Behind this door is a vestibule from which another door possibly leads into the tunnel. You can see this vestibule by peering through a louvred window in the men's lavatory in the Institute of Contemporary Arts, entered from the Mall. There is also thought to be another tunnel connecting the Duke of York's Steps with Buckingham Palace, although its existence has never been confirmed. It's supposed to have been constructed before or during the Second World War so that, in the event of an invasion, the royal family could make a quick getaway via Charing Cross tube station and Paddington main-line station to Bristol and so to Canada.

Before and during the war further 'citadels' were built outside the Whitehall district: for the Admiralty at Cricklewood; for the Air Ministry at Harrow; for the Cabinet Office under the Post Office Research Station at Dollis Hill; for MI5 under their building in Curzon Street, Mayfair; for the London civil defence organization next to the old Geological Museum (now part of the Natural History Museum) in South Kensington's Exhibition Road; and for the Post Office (now British Telecom, BT) next to the Faraday House telephone exchange in the City. All these citadels still exist, and the Admiralty citadel in Cricklewood was brought back into action in 1982 for the Falklands War.

Post Office cable tunnels

The government system links via the 'Q' Whitehall exchange tunnel with a 12-mile (19-kilometre) network of Post Office cable tunnels. Two tunnels fan out from Colombo House near Waterloo Station. One goes north-west to Trafalgar Square post office. The other goes north-east to the Faraday House telephone exchange in the City, between Blackfriars Bridge and London Bridge. The rest of the network is on the north bank and extends as far as

Shepherd's Bush in the west and Shoreditch in the east. Two-thirds of the network was built in the late 1940s and early 1950s in response to the Cold War atomic-bomb threat. The tunnels constructed at this time are over 16 feet (5 metres) in diameter and contain a 2-foot (60-centimetre) gauge railway for laying heavy cables. The later tunnels (the most recent of which, linking Paddington with Shepherd's Bush, was finished as late as 1976) are rather smaller. Access is through post offices and ordinary manhole covers like the one at the junction of Bethnal Green Road and Sclater Street in the East End. It used to be so easy to get into the tunnels that in 1980 the *New Statesman* magazine was able to hold its Christmas party in one!

The Post Office cable tunnels, now the responsibility of BT, connect with the Kingsway telephone exchange 100 feet (30 metres) down on either side of High Holborn under Chancery Lane Underground Station. Also built in the early 1950s in response to the atomic-bomb threat, its existence was almost completely unsuspected outside official circles until the late 1960s, even though it is directly beneath one of London's busiest streets. The exchange, which fills a number of interconnecting tunnels extending south down Furnival Street, is said to be so large that it takes as much as an hour and a half to walk round it. BT's large office at the eastern end of Holborn no doubt connects with it.

Deep-level shelters

Two of the tunnels in the Kingsway telephone exchange were originally built in 1942 to form the Chancery Lane deep-level shelter. This was one of eight such shelters, all beneath existing Underground stations and seven of them on the Northern Line. Each consisted of two parallel tunnels 1,200 feet (365 metres) long and divided into two floors. Four of the shelters (Belsize Park, Camden Town, Clapham North and Clapham South) were fitted with bunks for 8,000 people and used as public air-raid shelters. The other four were retained for government use. Chancery Lane and Clapham Common provided emergency citadels for use during V1 and V2 rocket attacks. Stockwell housed American troops and Goodge Street, linked to the Cabinet War Rooms by pneumatic despatch tube, became a subterranean D-Day communications centre for General Eisenhower, the Allied supreme commander.

Today the shelters still exist. Chancery Lane is part of the Kingsway exchange. The remaining seven shelters are all on the Northern Line and are identifiable on the surface by their distinctive blockhouse-type

Opposite: Deep below Chancery Lane Underground Station is a vast telephone exchange incorporating part of a Second World War emergency government citadel.

entrances. Three shelters (Belsize Park, Camden Town and Goodge Street) are used by a firm called Security Archives for storing commercial data. The remaining four (Stockwell, Clapham North, Clapham Common and Clapham South) are vacant. The leases for the shelters contain a clause that allows the government to reoccupy them should the need ever arise. Let us hope it does not.

UNDERGROUND RAILWAYS

During the 130 years of the existence of the Underground railway in London, some 40 stations above and below ground have become, for a variety of reasons, surplus to requirements. Fourteen below-ground stations still exist. The closest to central London is Down Street, just off Piccadilly near Hyde Park Corner. Opened on the Piccadilly Line in 1907, it was closed in 1932 because it was so close to both Hyde Park Corner and Green Park. During the Second World War it came into its own again when the government took it over as an emergency headquarters, equipping it with a telephone exchange, meeting rooms and living quarters. It was used mainly by the Railway Executive Committee, the organization responsible for co-ordinating the still private railways during the war years. But Churchill and his War Cabinet also used the centre occasionally during the Blitz, though their main base was of course the Cabinet War Rooms. Churchill's bath, near the stairs at the far end of the platform, is still in place, as is the old telephone exchange.

Today the station forms part of the Underground's ventilation system. At street level, the red-tiled façade is a typical example of Underground-station architecture in the early years of this century. Below ground, the only indication of the station's existence is a glimpse of a platform between Green Park and Hyde Park Corner.

King William Street
One of the most historic of the old stations is King William Street in the City. Opened in 1890, it was the northern terminus of the world's first electric tube railway, the City and South London Railway, which connected the City with Stockwell via a mile-long (1.6-kilometre) tunnel under the Thames. When this pioneering line was extended northwards to Moorgate in 1900, the engineers could not fit King William Street and its tunnel into the new system, and they unfortunately had to be abandoned. The station entrance was removed in 1933, but the platforms survived and were used during the war as an air-raid shelter. There are still old wartime posters on the walls.

'Passing Brompton Road'

Another ex-station with wartime relics is Brompton Road, opened in 1906 on the Piccadilly Line. Some trains were already passing straight through it by 1910 because two other Piccadilly Line stations (Knightsbridge and South Kensington) were so close. The guard's cry 'passing Brompton Road' became so well known (a bit like 'mind the gap' today) that it was adopted as the title of a popular West End play about commuting and the rat race. During the Second World War the station, which had closed in 1934, became the operations room of the Anti-Aircraft Command (not, as some books have it, an air-raid shelter). Below ground, the platforms have been walled off so you cannot see them from passing trains. One platform has a screen at one end on which films were shown during the war. At street level one of the original maroon-tiled entrances survives on the east side of Cottage Place, near the junction with Brompton Road.

Wood Lane

Wood Lane in Shepherd's Bush opened as a surface station on the overground section of the Metropolitan Line to serve the White City Franco-British exhibition of 1908. In 1920 two Underground platforms were added when the Central Line was extended from Shepherd's Bush to Ealing. But the station proved difficult for Central Line trains to use, so in 1947 a new Central Line station a little further up Wood Lane was built. This is the existing White City Underground Station. Wood Lane reverted to Metropolitan Line-only use and eventually closed in 1959. From Wood Lane itself you can see the station building with its name in relief above the entrance. The upper platforms are hidden behind high walls. Below ground, travelling east on the Central Line from White City to Shepherd's Bush, you pass one of the lower station platforms adorned with enamel nameplates and tattered posters that are half a century old.

North End

North End on the Northern Line was never actually opened as a station. Indeed, it was never even finished. After completing the platforms and short sections of the stairway, the Hampstead Tube Company abandoned the project in 1906 when Hampstead Heath was scheduled as a public open space and further suburban development in the immediate vicinity (the station's prospective market) scrapped. Had the station been completed, its entrance would have been at the junction of Hampstead Way and North End Road. Underground engineers tend to refer to it colloquially as Bull and Bush after the nearby pub of music-hall fame.

With its extreme depth – at 200 feet (60 metres) it's London's deepest Underground station – North End was given a new lease of life during the Cold War of the 1950s, when London Transport converted it into a control centre for activating the London Underground's floodgates in the event of a nuclear attack. That danger is long since perceived to have disappeared. Today the station is abandoned and the platforms are gone, but the site is visible from passing trains.

Disused tunnels

Besides disused Underground stations, London Underground also has several disused Underground tunnels. At New Cross there is a 472-foot (144-metre) tunnel built in 1971–2 for an uncompleted Jubilee Line extension to Thamesmead. Between St Pancras Station and a railway subterranean goods depot at Smithfield, there is a Metropolitan Line link abandoned after the war. Under the Thames there are three disused tunnels, all formerly part of the Northern Line. Two in the region of London Bridge form the abandoned double tunnel that used to carry the City and South London Railway from Borough Station to King William Street in the City. The third, between Hungerford Bridge and Blackfriars Bridge, formed the Northern Line's now abandoned Charing Cross loop. This was bombed during the war and is now flooded.

Mail Rail

London Underground is not the only organization to run underground railways in London. Besides the cable tunnel railway already mentioned, the Royal Mail also has its own tube railway, which it used for transporting sacks of mail between sorting offices and railway stations until 2003, when **Mail Rail**, as the railway was called, was decommissioned because it was proving too expensive to run.

When operating, Mail Rail ran from Paddington in the west to East London Sorting Office in Whitechapel, stopping en route at Liverpool Street railway station and several sorting offices, including Mount Pleasant. It was electrically operated, driverless and about the size of those miniature steam engines you can ride on at fun fairs and amusement parks. When it opened in 1927, it immediately took a quarter of London's mail vans off the roads, thus helping to reduce the traffic congestion that had prompted its construction in the first place. The 9-foot (3-metre) tunnels are 70 feet (21 metres) below ground, and it takes less than half an hour for one of the 34 trains on the circuit to travel all the way across London, including stops. In a van it would probably take three or four times that. The service is now mothballed pending a decision on its future.

TUNNELS UNDER THE THAMES

It has been calculated that there are well over 20 tunnels under the Thames, making it the most undermined capital river in the world. Besides the three disued tube tunnels and two Post Office cable tunnels already mentioned, there are nine tube tunnels, eight service tunnels, three road tunnels and two foot tunnels. The public tube, road and foot tunnels are, by definition, relatively well known; the service tunnels, which are closed to the public, are not.

Passing beneath the Thames between Barnes and Hammersmith in the west and Woolwich Reach in the east, these service tunnels mostly carry water mains and electricity cables. The most historically interesting is the Tower Subway running from Tower Hill next to the Tower of London to Vine Lane, Tooley Street, on the opposite bank. Opened in 1870, it was originally used by people crossing the Thames, first by 12-passenger cable car and then on foot. Following the opening of Tower Bridge in 1896, it was closed to the public and has not been reopened since.

Until the 1970s the Tower Subway was used by the London Hydraulic Power Company (see page 52) as a conduit for its mains. Now owned by Cable and Wireless Communications and the only privately owned tunnel under the Thames, it carries phone lines, cable TV and water mains. The tunnel is 7 feet (2 metres) in diameter.

UTILITY SUBWAYS

The public utilities have always been underground animals both because the earth cradles and protects their precious pipes and ducts and because there is nowhere for these conduits on the surface. For the most part the networks are buried in specially dug channels and trenches, but there are beneath London's streets several purpose-built service subways that enable maintenance and repair to be carried out without ripping up roads and pavements.

Altogether, there are nearly 12 miles (19 kilometres) of service subways in London, mainly underneath the West End, the City and Docklands. The principal system radiates out from Piccadilly Circus to Trafalgar Square, Shaftesbury Avenue, Regent Street, Charing Cross Road and Holborn. There is another subway in the vicinity of Holborn Viaduct and a third in the northern approaches to London Bridge around Arthur Street. There is also a little-known subway under the Kensington Court estate in west London. The longest is probably the one in the Embankment. It runs all the way from the Houses of Parliament to Blackfriars Bridge before turning inland to the Bank of England. The door at the base of the Boudicca statue on Westminster Bridge is the Westminster entrance.

Most of these subways, mainly designed to accommodate proliferating gas and water mains, were built as part of Victorian street-improvement schemes. The oldest subway, under Garrick Street in Covent Garden, was built in 1861. Far more modern is the circular tunnel that was built under Oxford Street in 1968 to contain services diverted by the modernization of Oxford Circus Underground. There are no signs on the surface that this tunnel exists, but the routes of the older subways are generally marked on pavements by the long, wide rectangular grids through which the heavy cast-iron pipes were inserted. Some of these pipes, still in excellent order, are 3 feet (1 metre) in diameter. One of the newest service subways in London is the complex of tunnels under Ludgate Hill near St Paul's, built in 1992 as a result of the lowering of the Snow Hill railway tunnel.

The London Hydraulic Power Company (LHPC)

The LHPC was founded in 1871 and for a hundred years supplied hydraulic power for heavy lifting machinery, including lifts and cranes, and safety curtains in West End theatres. In its heyday in the 1920s its network of mains carrying water at a pressure of 600 lb/square inch (42 kg/cm^2) spanned London from Limehouse in the east to Earl's Court in the west. The wonder is that it survived so long when electricity had more than come into its own as a source of power.

When the LHPC eventually ceased its century of operations in the 1970s, it bequeathed to the late 20th century a subterranean legacy of nearly 200 miles (320 kilometres) of 19th-century, 12-inch (30-centimetre) cast-iron pipes. A consortium including Rothschilds bought the network and has since occupied itself finding new uses for the pipes. As mentioned on page 51 in the description of the Tower Subway, Cable and Wireless Communications have taken over part of the system for their phone lines.

Giant waterworks

Virtually the entire water network in London is underground and therefore invisible. Could it but be brought to the surface and revealed in all its glory, it would be seen to be a marvel of engineering: beautiful brick-lined underground lakes with vaulted roofs (as at Putney Heath) and now, the latest feat of Thames Water, the London Tunnel Ring Main, a 50-mile (80-kilometre) bore 130 feet (40 metres) down and big enough to drive a car through. In fact in 1993 something approaching this actually happened when 10 cyclists rode along a 1.5-mile (2.5-kilometre) section of the tunnel as part of a charity bike race.

Completed in 1996, the ring main encircles London and supplies about half its water. Huge pump-out shafts big enough to put a bus in and extending right down to the main, bring up the water and channel it into local distribution systems. The closest one to central London is under the traffic island at the bottom of Park Lane, though you wouldn't know it from the surface.

Electrical network

As with water, much of London's electricity network is hidden from view, especially the small substations, of which there are 12,000, mostly invisible, strung out across the capital. These stations take power at 11,000 or 6,600 volts from larger converter stations and transform it down to 405 or 240 volts for distribution to individual customers.

One of the newest substations is bang underneath Leicester Square. Three storeys deep, it contains three large transformers and is entered via a large automatic trapdoor concealed in the pavement in the south-west corner of the square. The theatre ticket office in the square is also the ventilation extract shaft. A new mile-long (1.6-kilometre) tunnel, crossing four tube lines and passing 65 feet (20 metres) below Grosvenor Square, connects it with the ground-level Duke Street substation in Mayfair. In 1993–4, London Electricity built a new 6-mile (10-kilometre) tunnel between Pimlico and Wimbledon via Wandsworth to strengthen power supplies in south-west London.

The sewers

Last but not least in the reckoning of London's utilities with substantial underground structures is the capital's sewer system. Essentially this is another Victorian creation, and a particularly impressive and effective one at that. Its main feature is a series of large brick-lined tunnels running west to east on both sides of the Thames and parallel to it. These large tunnels, constructed with all the attention to design and detail so characteristic of the Victorian Age, intercept smaller sewers flowing north and south down towards the river and carry the effluent away to treatment works in east London (the northern one is at Beckton, and the southern is at Plumstead).

This very simple system, still performing well 140 years after its completion, was the brainchild of Sir Joseph Bazalgette, engineer to the Metropolitan Board of Works. The intercepts start out about 4 feet (1.2 metres) high and then gradually grow in size as they take in more tributary sewers. By the time they get to east London they are about 11 feet (3.5 metres) high. It is of course possible to walk around in the main intercepts, and people do (those whose job it is to keep the muck flowing and the structures themselves in good repair), but unfortunately they are never open to the public. Unlike the Paris sewers, which can be visited, London's sewers do not have raised walkways. Anyone venturing into them has to put on a pair of waders and take the plunge, which can be a dangerous business.

Although the sewers themselves are not open, you can at least visit two of the sewer system's magnificent, cathedral-like pumping stations: **Abbey Mills** on the north side of the river and **Crossness** on the south side. They have both been converted to electricity now, but Crossness still has its giant steam engines in situ and Abbey Mills is worth seeing for its superb ironwork.

SOME ONE-OFFS AND FAR-OUTS

The features of subterranean London described so far have generally been networks of tunnels and other types of buildings in the centre of the city. The ones that follow now are either one-offs or some distance from the city centre.

The Camden Town Catacombs, an extensive series of underground passageways and vaults lit via telltale cast-iron grilles in the road surface above, honeycomb the ground beneath the old canal–railway interchange at Camden Lock. They run from Camden Lock Market and the old Gilbey's gin warehouse next door, pass under the Primrose Hill goods yard and connect with a vast subterranean chamber that used to house the stationary steam winding engine that hauled trains up the incline into Euston main-line railway station. The catacombs were originally used for stabling ponies employed in shunting goods wagons in the yards above. Although disused, they are still railway property.

Underneath a former school behind Clerkenwell parish church on the northern fringes of the City is an amazing network of subterranean prison cells. They originally formed part of the Clerkenwell House of Detention, an overflow to the Bridewell women's prison a mile (1.6 kilometres) or so away beside the Thames. The Clerkenwell House of Detention was built in 1616 and the cells may well date back to that time, but it is more likely that they are a relic of a later rebuilding. For a while the cells formed part of the House of Detention museum, which is now closed.

Away out in east London there are two unknown tunnel systems. In Greenwich Park there is a series of what appears to be medieval brick-lined conduits west of the Royal Greenwich Observatory under the slope of the hill. No one knows exactly why they were built or when or, indeed, what for. The most common explanation is that they supplied water to the old royal palace of Placentia (no longer surviving), but that does not account for their large size: in parts they are like passageways and high enough for a person to walk through.

The Woolwich Arsenal system, extending from Thamesmead to Shooters Hill, dates from the 18th century and was once part of the enormous Royal Artillery/Royal Arsenal complex at Woolwich. Today it is used by the British Library as a bookstore.

Never outdone in anything, Harrods, the great emporium, of course has its own tunnel system. The main thoroughfare under the Brompton Road links the store with its warehouse (scheduled for conversion into a hotel) in Trevor Place. A network of smaller tunnels and cellars leading off it provide deep-freeze stores, wine cellars and last, but not least, a lock-up for shoplifters. Harrods is definitely not the place for claustrophobic kleptomaniacs.

In addition to four tube lines, the Thameslink tunnel, the Fleet Sewer, several gas mains and the London Tunnel Ring Main, the congested ground beneath King's Cross Station also envelops a pair of abandoned railway tunnels known as the 'York Road' and 'Hotel' curves. Linked to the main-line station by a ramped opening that gradually rises from a siding on the York Way side, these tunnels will probably be incorporated into the planned sub-ground enlargement of the main-line station and the construction of the new Channel Tunnel terminal.

Kingsway tram tunnel and more air-raid shelters

The Kingsway tram tunnel runs from Waterloo Bridge to Theobald's Road, via Aldwych and Kingsway. It was originally used by trams, but in the 1960s the southern section was converted into a traffic underpass as far as Holborn. The short section from Holborn to Theobald's Road, including the subterranean Theobald's Road tram station, was then used by the Greater London Council as its flood-control centre. The GLC has now gone and, with the building of the Thames Barrier, so has the imminent danger of flooding. The centre is now believed to have been abandoned.

To protect civilians caught outside by air raids in the Second World War, covered trench systems were built in many London squares and parks, including Hyde Park, Green Park, St James's Park, Queen Square, Woburn Square, Leicester Square, Russell Square, Bloomsbury Square and Lincoln's Inn Fields. The shelter in Lincoln's Inn Fields was nearly 1,500 feet (450 metres) long, 7 feet (2 metres) deep and roofed with concrete and 2 feet (60 centimetres) of earth. The Lincoln's Inn shelter and most of the others are believed still to exist, although the entrances have been blocked off. In Leicester Square the shelter was destroyed when the new electricity substation was built. The former entrance has survived half-way down the steps to the men's lavatory in the north-east corner of the square, but it now appears to have been sealed.

PRIVATE LANDOWNERS

One of the best-kept secrets in London is the fact that large chunks of the capital belong to historic estates that have been owned by the same institutions and families for hundreds of years – and, in the case of the Crown Estate, for nearly a thousand years. It is impossible to say precisely how much land is owned in this way. Landowners as a rule do not publicize the extent, or even the existence, of their estates, and there is nowhere you can go (such as a comprehensive public land registry, indexed by owner) to access this information. However, at the very least, the total (excluding parkland) must be something like 4,500 acres (1,800 hectares); in other words, getting on for seven times the size of the City.

Quite what all this must be worth to the fortunate owners in question is impossible to compute. As an indication, the value of the Queen's central London property (in the City, West End, Regent's Park and Kensington, excluding parkland) is currently put at over £1 billion (US$1.5 billion).

Traditional landowners own most of their property freehold and make their money from letting it to leaseholders for a fixed term of years. Leaseholders may in turn sublet to an occupier, or even to another leaseholder. Sometimes there are whole chains of leaseholders between freeholders and occupiers, an arrangement which makes it even more difficult to establish who owns what. To take one conspicuous but relatively simple example: the Queen is the freeholder of Spencer House in St James's; Earl Spencer, brother of the late Princess of Wales, is the head leaseholder; and Lord Rothschild's St James's Place Capital plc is the sub-leaseholder and occupier.

THE CITY

The City Corporation owns nearly a third of the City's 677 acres (274 hectares) in its twin guises of private landowner and government-appointed local authority. In its local-authority role, it owns a 115-acre (46-hectare) 'Planning Estate' mainly acquired after the Second World War to expedite the rebuilding of blitzed areas like the Barbican. In its private capacity, the corporation owns two historic estates whose origins go way back to the beginnings of the modern City in the early Middle Ages.

The larger of the two is the so-called 'City's Cash' estate. The Cash estate derives originally from the City's ancient right to acquire any 'wastes and open spaces' in the City. Today it owns land both in and outside the City. The core holding is the 35-acre (14-hectare) estate actually in the Square Mile. This includes the Old Bailey, parts of New Broad Street, Whitefriars and Fenchurch Street and the City's two surviving markets, Smithfield and Leadenhall. Outside the City, the Cash estate also owns two relocated City markets – the Spitalfields fruit and vegetable market, now in Leyton and the Billingsgate fish market, now in Docklands. It also owns a 27-acre (11-hectare) Mayfair estate called Conduit Mead.

Conduit Mead

Conduit Mead has an interesting history. In the 17th century it was a Tyburn-side field that the City leased from the Crown so that it could draw water from a spring in the field. Then in 1628 King Charles I, gearing up for his 11-year rule without parliament and therefore taxes, needed to obtain money from the City. The City Corporation duly obliged with the cash and received the freehold of Conduit Mead in return. From the 18th century the estate was developed with houses. Today it is bisected by New Bond Street and takes in all or part of Brook Street, Maddox Street, Grafton Street, Conduit Street and South Molton Street. Since these streets are now among the most fashionable and expensive in London, the estate should by rights be netting the City an extremely healthy annual income. Unfortunately, this is not quite the case. The original leases, granted in 1754, had to be 'perpetually renewable' in order to attract tenants. This means that, despite the huge increase in the value of the property that has taken place since then, all holders of the leases have been able to renew them endlessly at the original 18th-century rent. So today it is the lease-holders and not the City who are making all the money. They will continue to do so for centuries to come. The 1925 Property Act did reduce 'perpetually' to 2,000 years maximum, but that still leaves another 1,800 years to go before the City can get its hands on Conduit Mead again and bump up the rent to more realistic levels. Meanwhile the City's presence in Mayfair can be seen most clearly in South Molton Street, where its red-and-white coat of arms has been fixed to the fronts of Nos 13, 44 and 65 (the latter painted over) and where the blue plaque to the poet William Blake at No. 17 is of the distinctive square City type rather than the usual circular sort.

In total, the Cash estate brings into the City a reasonably respectable £70 million (US$105 million) a year. A large slice of this money goes straight out again to maintain the largest part (in area) of the Cash estate, namely

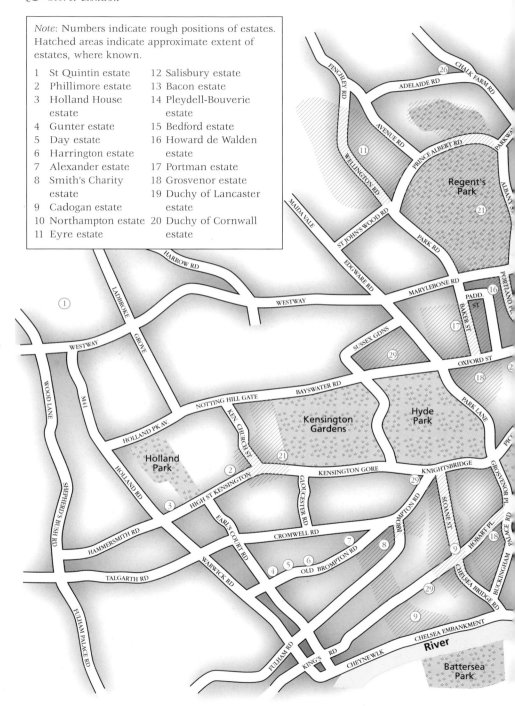

Note: Numbers indicate rough positions of estates. Hatched areas indicate approximate extent of estates, where known.

1 St Quintin estate
2 Phillimore estate
3 Holland House estate
4 Gunter estate
5 Day estate
6 Harrington estate
7 Alexander estate
8 Smith's Charity estate
9 Cadogan estate
10 Northampton estate
11 Eyre estate
12 Salisbury estate
13 Bacon estate
14 Pleydell-Bouverie estate
15 Bedford estate
16 Howard de Walden estate
17 Portman estate
18 Grosvenor estate
19 Duchy of Lancaster estate
20 Duchy of Cornwall estate

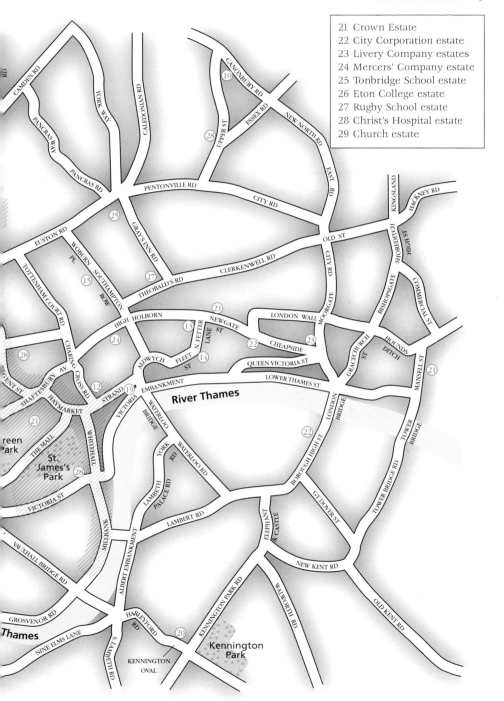

21 Crown Estate
22 City Corporation estate
23 Livery Company estates
24 Mercers' Company estate
25 Tonbridge School estate
26 Eton College estate
27 Rugby School estate
28 Christ's Hospital estate
29 Church estate

the 9,000 acres (3,650 hectares) of forests, common and open spaces in and around London, acquired since 1878 specifically for the recreation of cooped-up city dwellers. The largest is the 6,000-acre (2,400-hectare) Epping Forest, north-east of London. Also in the portfolio are West Ham Park, Highgate Wood and Queen's Park. The newest addition is Hampstead Heath, taken over from the defunct Greater London Council in 1989. All these properties are non-income generating and are hugely expensive to keep up: the 800-acre (320-hectare) Hampstead Heath, for example, costs anywhere up to £4 million (US$6 million) a year to look after.

Bridge House Estates

The City Corporation's other historic landholding goes by the name of the Bridge House Estates. This estate consists of land given or bequeathed in the Middle Ages and later for the maintenance of old London Bridge, completed in 1201. The last bequest was in 1675. Most of the land is south of the river in areas like Borough High Street and Hay's Wharf, which were opened up by the construction of London Bridge and later bridges across the Thames.

The income from the estates was, and still is, used for building and maintaining the bridges across the Thames owned by the City. There are four of these – London Bridge, Blackfriars Bridge, Southwark Bridge and Tower Bridge – but the estate has actually paid for six: the medieval London Bridge's two replacements, 1831 and 1972; the new Blackfriars Bridge, 1869 (the 1769 original was paid for mainly with money from another source); the two Southwark Bridges, 1819 and 1921; and Tower Bridge, completed in 1894. Today there is over £300 million (US$450 million) in the Bridge House kitty, which is growing at the rate of £20 million (US$30 million) a year. City officials are naturally wondering what to do with the surplus: a new bridge to ease the pressure on Tower Bridge is one option under consideration.

THE LIVERY COMPANIES

The long-established livery companies (see pages 140-6) are another major traditional landowner in London, particularly in the City. Nobody knows exactly what or how much they own, but a mid-1980s' estimate put their property in the Square Mile alone at 15 per cent of the total City area, in other words about 100 acres (40 hectares).

Most livery-company property consists of livery halls and the surrounding land. Between them, the Carpenters and the Drapers own all of Throgmorton Avenue, where both have their halls. Just to the west the Drapers own a great swathe of land stretching back from Throgmorton Street to London Wall, which was once their garden (hence the street

Drapers Gardens running through the middle), and another block in St Swithin's Lane where their first hall stood. To the east, the Leathersellers own every freehold around their hall in St Helen's Place, and more either side in Bishopsgate and St Mary Axe. To the west, the Grocers own nearly all of the west side of Prince's Street around Grocers' Hall Gardens, opposite the Bank of England, plus more land in Cornhill and Old Jewry. To the south, the Merchant Taylors at 30 Threadneedle Street have since the 14th century owned virtually everything on their island site bounded by Finch Lane, Cornhill and Bishopsgate.

Of course, the livery companies also own plenty of property in London outside the City. The Mercers, for example, rumoured to be the biggest landowners of all the livery companies, have an estate in Covent Garden around Mercer Street. And the Goldsmiths have 200 acres (80 hectares) of Ealing, left to them by a member called John Perryn in 1657. Much of the estate consists of playing fields. There also an impressive range of almshouses built in 1811.

Public school landowners

Several livery companies have close connections with long-established public schools, and in one case at least the school has an old London estate that is still managed for it by its sponsoring livery company. In 1553 Sir Andrew Judd, Muscovy merchant and member of the Skinners' Company, founded a school in his home town of Tonbridge in Kent and endowed it with an estate in St Pancras. That estate is now around Tonbridge Street, Cartwright Gardens and the top end of Judd Street, near St Pancras Station, and it is still looked after by the Skinners' Company. Hence the Skinners Arms pub at 114 Judd Street.

Besides Tonbridge, several other old public schools have estates in London. Eton College in Windsor owns the 60-acre (24-hectare) Chalcot estate north of Primrose Hill. Formerly a farm, it was given to the school by King Henry VI, founder of Eton in 1440. Today it can be identified by street names such as Eton Villas, Provost Road and King Henry's Road. Rugby School in Warwickshire was founded in 1567 with an estate around what is now Rugby Street, close to the famous children's hospital in Great Ormond Street, WC1. The land on which the hospital stands was bought from the school, so reducing the original 8-acre (3-hectare) endowment somewhat. Today the school, having missed the boat on development, is saddled with huge bills for maintaining its inheritance of handsome 18th-century listed houses, so there may not be a Rugby estate in the area for much longer.

The Rugby estate includes the northern section of Lamb's Conduit Street. The southern section, along with Dombey Street, Emerald Street and part of Bedford Row, belongs to the Harper estate, the endowment of Bedford School founded by William Harper in 1566. This estate was originally 13 acres (5 hectares) in extent, but it has now shrunk to 3 acres (1.2 hectares). Probably the largest old school estate in central London belongs to Christ's Hospital. Besides land in Soho, Islington and Westminster (most of Queen Anne's Gate, where the National Trust is based, Old Queen Street and Carteret Street), it includes the freehold of two West End theatres (the Queen's and the Gielgud in Shaftesbury Avenue) and an industrial estate in the East End. The school, now based in Horsham, West Sussex, was originally founded in the City by King Edward VI in 1553. Today its wealth is such that all but six of its 800-plus pupils are on subsidized fees.

The largest old school estate in Greater London must be that belonging to Dulwich College in south London. The school's founder, actor Edward Alleyn, endowed it with the 1,500-acre (600-hectare) manor of Dulwich in 1619. Today the manor remains virtually intact (although Dulwich Park has been acquired by the local authority), and with its woodlands and large open spaces has all the appearance of a country, rather than an urban, estate. Through the middle runs a College-owned road that is barred half-way by the last toll gate in London. The revenue is about £20,000 (US$30,000) a year. In the centre of Dulwich village is the school's public **picture gallery** with its world-famous collection of Old Masters.

CHURCH ESTATES

You may have noticed that, with the exception of Eton, all these schools were endowed around the same time, that is to say in the 1550s and 1560s. The reason for this is that, during the Middle Ages, the monasteries ran the schools. When the monasteries were dissolved as part of the Protestant Reformation in the middle of the 1500s, other ways of funding schools had to be found: endowing them with their own estates was the obvious method, since that is how monasteries also had been supported.

Although the monasteries lost their estates during the Reformation, the rest of the Church clung on to its extensive landholdings. Today these estates, managed since 1948 by church commissioners, generate income that mainly goes towards paying clergy stipends. Once upon a time the Church of England's estate in London, handed down from bishop of London to bishop of London, covered hundreds of acres, but this century it has considerably diminished in size.

The largest single block today is the Hyde Park estate, a 90-acre (40-hectare) triangle of upmarket houses between Sussex Gardens, Edgware

Road and Bayswater Road. Originally developed from 1827 onwards with increasingly large stuccoed terraces, much of this area has been rebuilt since the 1950s with more manageable town houses. This has enabled it to retain its social cachet and therefore its value to the Church. Elsewhere in London, in places like Brixton, Lambeth, Vauxhall and Stoke Newington, the Church owns the Octavia Hill housing estates. Unlike the Hyde Park estate, which is purely an investment, these fulfil a social purpose by providing homes for people on small incomes who need to live in central London. As well as residential property, the Church also has an extensive commercial property portfolio in London, though to what extent this is the result of the development of historic estates or modern property dealing is not clear. Some of the more conspicuous commercial premises are the Royal Lancaster Hotel at Lancaster Gate (the western corner of the Hyde Park estate), offices at 107–169 Victoria Street and shops in Connaught Street (also on the Hyde Park estate), Knightsbridge (55–91) and King's Road, Chelsea (virtually every one between 195 and 277).

THE CROWN ESTATE

Historically, the Church and the Crown were the two biggest landowners in London. But whereas the Church has either lost or disposed of most of its property (one recent disposal was its historic estate in Maida Vale, where it is believed Harrow School also has an estate), the Crown has managed to hang on to its possessions so that today it is far and away the largest historic landowner in London.

The official **Crown Estate** consists essentially of 12 million – yes, 12 million – square feet (over 1.1 million square metres) of commercial space, mainly shops and offices, in central London, and over 1,000 acres (400 hectares), mainly residential land and golf clubs, in outer London. Not part of the official Crown Estate but still royal property are the 5,000 acres (2,000 hectares) of parkland in both central and outer London, and the small Duchy of Cornwall and Duchy of Lancaster estates.

Central London

With one significant exception, most of the central London Crown Estate is described either as 'ancient possession', which means it has been owned by the Crown for as long as there have been records (i.e. approaching 1,000 years), or was acquired during the 16th century. As an example of the latter, Regent's Park, originally part of Barking Abbey's manor of Tyburn, was appropriated by the rapacious Henry VIII in 1544 following the closure of the monastery and the seizure of its property.

63

The 'significant exception' is Regent Street: although a major part of the central London estate today with nearly a quarter of the Crown's commercial space in London, it was not acquired until the early 19th century. Its purchase was made necessary by John Nash's ambitious scheme to link Regent's Park with Carlton House, the Prince Regent's palace overlooking St James's Park.

The core of the Crown Estate in London is a broad and virtually continuous strip of land between Primrose Hill in the north and Millbank/Victoria Street in the south. Broken only by Portland Place, the strip follows Regent Street, Haymarket, Trafalgar Square and Whitehall. Among other things it includes the gleaming stucco terraces of Regent's Park and Carlton House Terrace (where the Crown Estate Commissioners have their office); all the famous shops like Liberty and Mappin & Webb on both sides of Regent Street; Piccadilly Circus and its lights; the clubs, art dealers and Green Park-facing mansions of St James's; cinemas and theatres in Haymarket, including the Theatre Royal; and the two large buildings facing each other across Trafalgar Square, Canada House and South Africa House. The Crown Estate also includes a clutch of big West End hotels like the Intercontinental, the Inn on the Park, Le Meridien Piccadilly and the Strand Palace.

In the City, the Crown Estate has over a million square feet (100,000 square metres) of office space, mainly blocks of offices in Holborn Viaduct, Cornhill, East Smithfield (Royal Mint Court) and Leadenhall Street. Away to the west, the Kensington estate is made up of two components: first, the individual mansions in Kensington Palace Gardens and Palace Green, now mostly used as embassies; and, second, half a million-plus square feet (50,000 square metres) of shops and offices in lucrative Kensington High Street, including the former Derry & Toms department store, with its large roof garden (see page 164).

Greater London

In outer London, almost all the 1,000-plus acres (400 hectares) of houses and golf clubs are divided between Eltham and Richmond. Eltham in south-east London, an ancient possession where the remains of the royal palace can still be seen, has 490 acres (200 hectares). The golf clubs are the Royal Blackheath and Eltham Warren. Richmond in south-west London, another ancient possession where again the remains of the royal palace can be seen, has 375 acres (150 hectares), including the Old Deer Park and the Royal Mid-Surrey Golf Club between Kew and Richmond.

Opposite: The famous 'lights' of Piccadilly Circus were opposed by the London County Council when the first ones were put up in the early 20th century.

In Richmond itself, Richmond Park is, at 2,470 acres (1,000 hectares), by far the largest royal park in London. Then come in descending order of magnitude: Bushy Park and Hampton Court Park, 1,099 acres (445 hectares); Hyde Park and Kensington Gardens, 615 acres (250 hectares); Regent's Park, 420 acres (170 hectares); Greenwich Park, 200 acres (80 hectares); Primrose Hill Park, 112 acres (45 hectares); St James's Park, 90 acres (36 hectares); and Green Park, 53 acres (21 hectares).

Duchies of Lancaster and Cornwall estates

The Crown Estate is really semi-public property, for all its income (minus management expenses) is surrendered to the government in return for a royal family operating grant known as the Civil List. The estates of the Duchies of Lancaster and Cornwall, however, are very much personal possessions, and the Queen is entitled to keep every penny they earn. Both these estates are mainly agricultural and therefore mainly outside London, but each has its central London nucleus.

The Duchy of Lancaster's London estate consists of 3 or 4 acres (1–1.5 hectares) under and around the Savoy Hotel in WC2 and essentially covers the site of the medieval palace of Savoy, home of royal Earls and Dukes of Lancaster in the 13th and 14th centuries. The land has always been Crown property except for a brief period in the mid-13th century when it was granted to Queen Eleanor's uncle, the Count of Savoy, and then bequeathed by him to the monastery of St Bernard in Savoie in 1268. Queen Eleanor bought it back in 1270 and gave it to her second son, Edmund, Earl of Lancaster. Today the only surviving part of the palace is the Savoy Chapel in Savoy Street. The estate is managed from the duchy office in Lancaster Place.

The 45-acre (18-hectare) Duchy of Cornwall estate is south of the river in the Kennington area. Though it has some shops and offices, it mainly consists of 600 flats and houses – mostly let on low rents, often to ex-royal family employees – and the 10-acre (4-hectare) Oval cricket ground, on long lease to Surrey County Cricket Club. Ever since 1337, when Edward III created his eldest son Duke of Cornwall, the income from the estate has been used to support the heir to the throne. Prince Charles is the 25th Duke of Cornwall: he receives three-quarters of the income and gives the rest – maybe as much as £500,000 (US$750,000) a year – to the government. The duchy is managed from an elegant office at 10 Buckingham Gate with a panelled first-floor boardroom known as the Prince's Council Chamber.

NON-ROYAL ESTATES

Below the royal family, at least a dozen non-royal families own substantial historic estates in London. Three of the largest holdings are in the lucrative West End and have helped put their owners – worth collectively about £4.3 billion (US$6.5 billion) according to one recent survey – high in the ranks of the wealthiest men in Britain. Indeed, the owner of the largest of these estates, Gerald Grosvenor, 6th Duke of Westminster, is said to be the richest commoner in the country. It is also said that his estate has an asset value equivalent to that of the eighth largest company in the UK.

The Grosvenor estate

Although the Grosvenors were an ancient Norman family who came over to England either with William the Conqueror in 1066 or not long after, they were mere country gentlemen in Cheshire until a fortuitous marriage in 1677 brought them 300 acres (120 hectares) of boggy farmland on the western fringe of London. Careful development of that land in the 18th and 19th centuries, besides catapulting the family into the peerage stratosphere, created the districts we know today as Mayfair, Belgravia and Pimlico. From the beginning, Mayfair and Belgravia have been two of the smartest addresses in London, but Pimlico, south of Victoria Station, degenerated before and after the Second World War into a seedy area of slums and brothels. Embarrassed by the frequency with which his name was figuring in prosecutions of brothel-keepers, the 2nd Duke sold Pimlico in 1950 and invested the money overseas, primarily in Vancouver.

The Mayfair estate, around 100 acres (40 hectares) with roughly 1,500 properties, stretches from Park Lane across to South Molton Lane and Avery Row and from Oxford Street down to South Street and Bruton Place. In the middle is Grosvenor Square, one of the largest squares in London. The whole of the west side is taken up by the US Embassy; it's the only US embassy in the world where the USA does not own the freehold.

The Grosvenor estate in Belgravia, about 200 acres (80 hectares) with roughly 3,000 properties, takes in all the land between Knightsbridge and Ebury Bridge Road/Buckingham Palace Road, and between Sloane Street/Chelsea Bridge Road and Grosvenor Place, except for a thinnish strip up the side of Sloane Street. The centrepiece of Belgravia is Belgrave Square, although Eaton Square to the south is also a prominent feature.

Both Mayfair and Belgravia were built as residential areas, but today only a third of the former and half the latter are lived in. The majority of the houses have been taken over by firms and embassies seeking central locations and prestigious addresses.

The Grosvenor estate, operating from the **Grosvenor estate office** at 70–72 Grosvenor Street in Mayfair, exercises strict control over the appearance of its properties. Satellite dishes, for example, are not allowed, and all stucco exteriors have to be regularly painted in a special kind of magnolia paint. The estate also adopts a far higher public profile than any other private landlord in London. There are places (such as Kinnerton Street in Belgravia) where you can see 'Grosvenor Estate' signs and wheatsheaf plaques fixed to the walls of some of the houses: the wheatsheaf is the main feature of the Grosvenor coat of arms. There are even walking guides to Mayfair and Belgravia, published by the estate, which accurately delineate the extent of the Grosvenors' London property. Neither the City nor the Crown goes this far.

Portman estate

Immediately north of the Grosvenors' Mayfair estate is the 110-acre (45-hectare) Portman estate, centred on Portman Square and bounded by Crawford Street, Oxford Street, Edgware Road and Manchester Square. Given to Lord Chief Justice Portman by Henry VIII back in 1533, this is possibly the oldest private estate in London. The owner today is Christopher, 10th Viscount Portman, who lives on a 3,000-acre (1,200-hectare) estate at Clifford in Herefordshire.

Howard de Walden estate

Adjoining the Portman estate on its east side is the Howard de Walden estate. This also covers 110 acres (45 hectares) and occupies all the land between Marylebone Road and Wigmore Street, and from Marylebone High Street to Great Portland Street. In the early 18th century the estate was owned by the Harleys, Earls of Oxford, hence Harley Street. From them it passed to the Dukes of Portland. In 1879 the 5th Duke died unmarried and his sister brought it into the Howard de Walden family. The owners today – along with 3,000 acres (1,200 hectares) in Berkshire – are the four daughters of the 9th and last Baron Howard de Walden who died in 1999. There are 1,200 houses on the estate, all of which have planning permission for use as offices, so very few of them are actually lived in. The estate is run from an office at 23 Queen Anne Street. You can find out more about it from the estate's own magazine, *The Marylebone Journal*, available in local libraries.

Bedford estate

Still moving east, the next old family estate to be encountered is the Bedford estate, a much-reduced 20-acre (8-hectare) holding in the British

Museum area. One part is in and around Bedford Square, London's finest surviving Georgian square. The other is in the Russell Square area between Montague Street and Bedford Row. Henry Russell, Marquess of Tavistock and heir to the 13th Duke of Bedford, is owner of this estate, plus 13,000 acres (5,300 hectares) of Bedfordshire around Woburn Abbey. He reluctantly inherited in 1974 when his father went to live in Monte Carlo as a tax exile. The Russells acquired the property as a result of Lord William Russell's marriage to the Earl of Southampton's daughter in 1669.

Small estates in the Covent Garden/Fleet Street area

South of the Bedford estate are three smaller family estates in the Covent Garden/Fleet Street area, the sizes of which are unknown. The western-most, incorporating Cecil Court between St Martin's Lane and Charing Cross Road, belongs to the Cecils, Marquesses of Salisbury, a family that first rose to prominence under Elizabeth I in the late 1500s. William Cecil and his son Robert, the 1st Earl of Salisbury, were both chief ministers to the queen. Lord Salisbury acquired the estate in 1609 and 1610. Development began at once: first the west side of St Martin's Lane, then Leicester Square, then the ground in between. Today the property is much reduced in size. The present owner is Robert Cecil, the 6th Marquess. Born in 1916, he lives at Hatfield House, a massive Elizabethan mansion just off the A1 north of London. His heir, Viscount Cranborne, lives at Cranborne on the family's 13,000-acre (5,300-hectare) Dorset estate. In early 1994 an amusing incident occurred when, during an altercation in a restaurant on Cecil Lane, an irate waiter said to Lord Valentine Cecil: 'Do you think you own this place?' In response, Lord Valentine is reported to have merely smiled – and nodded.

Going east, the next estate is the tiny Colville estate in the heart of legal London. Bounded by Southampton Buildings and Rolls Passage on the east side of Chancery Lane, it was acquired 400 years ago by Sir Nicholas Bacon, a prominent lawyer and Lord Keeper of the Great Seal under Elizabeth I. One of Bacon's sons was Sir Francis Bacon, philosopher and Lord Chancellor. Another was created premier baronet of England in 1611. It is the baronet's descendant, Sir Nicholas, the 14th Baronet and a lawyer like his ancestors, who owns the estate today. Besides the Colville estate, Sir Nicholas also owns 14,000 acres (5,660 hectares) of Norfolk at Raveningham, where he lives, and a further 9,000 acres (3,600 hectares) in Lincolnshire.

Across Fleet Street from the Colville estate, the Pleydell-Bouveries, Earls of Radnor, have a small estate in and around Bouverie Street in the heart of the old Fleet Street newspaper quarter. The estate once owned the Harmsworth House and Northcliffe House West newspaper offices. The Bouverie family came from the Château des Bouveries near Lille in Flanders in the 16th century and established themselves in London as merchants trading with Turkey. A baronetcy came in 1714 and then the earldom of Radnor in 1765. It was at about this time that they are believed to have bought the London estate. Today Jacob, the 8th Earl, lives on the 10,000-acre (4,000-hectare) Longford Castle estate near Salisbury surrounded by a fabulous picture collection. It is his son and heir, Viscount Folkestone, who actually owns the London estate (and a large chunk of the south-coast port of Folkestone as well).

North London family estates

On the northern fringes of London there are two old family estates, one in Islington and one in St John's Wood. The Canonbury estate in Islington, now centred on Canonbury Square, originally belonged to the Priory of St Bartholomew in Smithfield. After the closure of the priory, it was bought by John Spencer, later Lord Mayor of London. His daughter and heiress Elizabeth married the Earl of Northampton. Four hundred years later, the owner is Spencer Compton, the five-times-married 7th Marquess of Northampton. Lord Northampton lives at Compton Wynyates, the picture-book Tudor manor house in Warwickshire. He has another fine house and estate at Castle Ashby in Northamptonshire. The full extent of the Islington estate is unknown.

On the far side of the Fleet valley from Islington, the Eyre family, based on the Sadborow estate in Chard, Somerset, owns a substantial estate of about 130 acres (55 hectares) in the expensive residential district of St John's Wood, north of Regent's Park. It stretches from Lord's up to Belsize Road and across from Abbey Road to Avenue Road. City wine merchant Henry Eyre, brother of the Lord Chief Justice, bought the estate for £20,000 from Lord Chesterfield of *Letters* fame in 1732. At that time it covered nearly 500 acres (200 hectares) of farmland. His descendants started developing it about 1815, prompted by John Nash's work in nearby Regent's Park.

Two houses in Norfolk Road (Nos 15 and 16) dating from this period are the oldest surviving semi-detached houses in London. Lord's Cricket Ground was laid out by Thomas Lord on 8 acres (3 hectares) of land leased from the estate in 1814. The MCC eventually acquired the freehold in 1866. On the opposite side of the estate, the Board of Ordnance leased some land in 1820 and built a new barracks on it, together with a fine riding school and officers' mess. Today the modernized barracks, incorporating the Georgian riding school and mess, are home to the King's Troop, Royal Horse Artillery, which fires official salutes in Hyde Park on the Queen's birthday and other occasions.

KENSINGTON AND CHELSEA

In one west London borough – Kensington and Chelsea – at least nine historic estates survive.

Cadogan estate

Kensington and Chelsea stretches all the way up from the River Thames just west of Westminster to the Harrow Road north of Notting Hill. In the southern part 90 acres (37 hectares) of fashionable Chelsea belong to the Cadogan estate, the property of Earl Cadogan, who lives at 7 Smith Street SW3, and his eldest son, Viscount Chelsea. The Cadogans, originally from Wales, also have estates in Oxfordshire and Perthshire. They acquired Chelsea in 1717 when a soldier ancestor, Charles Cadogan, married the daughter of wealthy physician Sir Hans Sloane, benefactor of the British Museum and, more to the point, Chelsea's lord of the manor. Eighty per cent residential, the Cadogan estate is today quite fragmented. The main block, including Sloane Street and Cadogan Square, stretches from Knightsbridge down to below Sloane Square. West, there are other blocks both sides of the King's Road as far as Beaufort Street.

Smith's Charity estate

Abutting the Cadogan estate on the north side of Fulham Road and Walton Street is the 58-acre (24-hectare) **Smith's Charity estate**, acquired for £2,000 under the will of Alderman Henry Smith, who died in 1628. Smith's aim in financing the posthumous purchase of the land (then market gardens and farmland) was to raise money to ransom English seamen captured and enslaved by Barbary pirates, and to support such of his poor relations as could not earn their own living. By the 18th century the Barbary pirates no longer posed a threat, so from 1772 all the income from the estate was handed out among the neediest of his descendants.

In the 19th century, when the estate was developed into a prime residential area and started producing serious money, the aims of the charity were amended again to allow most of the income to be devoted to proper charitable projects, such as medical research. As late as 1992, however, Smith's 'poor kindred' were still receiving nearly £200,000 a year from the estate. In 1995 Smith's Charity sold out to the medical charity Wellcome Trust for the huge sum of £280 million (US$410 million). The old Smith's Charity estate stretches from Harrods west to Evelyn Gardens. You can get a history and plan of it from the estate office at 48 Pelham Street near South Kensington Underground Station.

Alexander estate

In between South Kensington Underground Station and the Smith's Charity estate is the Alexander estate. Originally this covered 54 acres (22 hectares). It is believed to be much smaller than this now, but it still includes Alexander Square and Thurloe Square directly opposite the Victoria & Albert Museum.

The estate is commonly believed to have been given by Oliver Cromwell to his secretary of state, John Thurloe, but it is more likely that a grandson of Thurloe's married the heiress of the property, Anna Maria Harris, in the early 18th century. At the end of the century, the then owner left it to a fortunate godson named John Alexander. A century later, after the Alexander family had developed it, an Alexander girl married a Campbell, one of the sons of the Duke of Argyll, bringing the estate with her. A descendant of that marriage, Ian Fife Campbell Anstruther, owns the estate today. He lives at 13 Thurloe Square.

Harrington estate

Immediately to the west of the Alexander estate, in the Stanhope Gardens/ Harrington Gardens area, Charles Stanhope, Viscount Petersham, heir to the 11th Earl of Harrington, owns the 12-acre (5-hectare) residue of the Harrington estate. The Harringtons acquired the estate in the 18th century when the 3rd Earl married one of the daughters of Sir John Fleming, who died in 1763.

Lord Petersham also owns a country estate at Westbury in Wiltshire, and his father lives on a 700-acre (280-hectare) stud farm in County Limerick, Eire. The family used to have a castle at Elvaston in Derbyshire. There are both Elvaston and Petersham street names on the part of the estate north of the Cromwell Road, which is believed to have been sold.

The Day estate

Bordering the Harrington estate to the south is the Day estate. This spans Old Brompton Road west of its junction with Gloucester Road and includes Hereford Square, Wetherby Place, Rosary Gardens and the northern section of Drayton Gardens, named after the village of Drayton near Norwich, where some of the Days lived in the 1830s. Originally 13 acres (over 5 hectares) in extent, the estate is now quite a bit smaller following sales such as the one in 1972, when 28 properties were disposed of. The land came into the Day family after Benjamin Day, a mercer in Covent

Opposite: The east wing of early 17th-century Holland House in Holland Park is the only surviving part of Kensington's one-time manor house.

Garden, married the daughter of a neighbour named Walter Dodemead, who had himself acquired it when he foreclosed on a mortgage in 1735. Simon Day is the owner of the estate today.

The Gunter estate

West of the Day estate is the Gunter estate in Earl's Court and West Brompton. Originally the estate covered over 100 acres (40 hectares), but much of the land was sold in 1917. The founder of the Gunter family fortunes was Robert Gunter, proprietor of Gunter's Tea Shop in Berkeley Square, one of the great institutions of Regency London. George III bought his buns there, and the aristocracy of Mayfair lounged about outside on hot days cooling themselves with Gunter's renowned ices and sorbets. As well as creating a successful catering business, which is still going under the name of Payne & Gunter, Gunter also bought land in Kensington, between Barkstone Gardens and Wetherby Gardens in the north and Gunter Grove and Edith Grove in the south. The profits from the development of this land, starting with the Boltons in the 1850s, enabled the Gunters to acquire a large estate near Wetherby, North Yorkshire. They lived there until Sir Ronald, the 3rd and last Baronet, died in 1980. His daughters and grandchildren have no doubt inherited the property.

Holland House estate

Across Kensington High Street from the Gunter estate, Charlotte Townshend, daughter of Lord Galway, owns what is left of the Holland House estate. Originally the estate comprised 200 acres (80 hectares), but sales over the years have reduced it, particularly the disposal in 1951 of 52 acres (21 hectares) of gardens and parkland surrounding the bombed-out remains of Holland House. These remains, incorporating a youth hostel, can still be seen in the middle of Holland Park, which is now a public open space (see page 14).

Mrs Townshend also owns a 3,000-acre (1,200-hectare) estate in Nottinghamshire and a 15,000-acre (6,000-hectare) estate around Melbury House near Dorchester, Dorset, where she lives. She inherited Melbury and the Holland estate from the Earls of Ilchester, who in turn acquired it from their cousins the Hollands in the 19th century. The 1st Lord Holland, father of rake and politician Charles James Fox, originally bought the estate in 1768.

Phillimore estate

To the east of Holland Park is an estate belonging to Lord Phillimore. His ancestors acquired the land through the marriage of Joseph Phillimore, a

Gloucestershire clothier's son, to Ann D'Oyley, daughter of a wealthy City merchant, in 1704. Originally 64 acres (26 hectares) but now much reduced, the estate covers the southern slope of Campden Hill and is made up of brilliant white stucco terraces in streets like Phillimore Walk and Phillimore Place. In 1874 artist and *Punch* cartoonist Edward Linley Sambourne leased one of these houses – then virtually new – and lived in it for the rest of his life. His family kept it unchanged after his death and it is now a fascinating Victorian time-capsule **museum**. Lord Phillimore, who is the 5th Baron, lives at Binfield Heath, near Henley, in Oxfordshire.

St Quintin estate

In the remote northern part of the borough, near the canal and the railway lines, the Legard family of Scampston Hall near Malton in North Yorkshire owns the very small remains of the 200-acre (80-hectare) St Quintin estate in the vicinity of St Quintin Avenue. The St Quintin family, Yorkshire squires since the Middle Ages, acquired the estate in the form of a farm called Notting Barns in 1767. The farm was developed in the 19th century, and many of the freeholds were then sold off in the 20th century. Lady Legard of Scampston Hall is the daughter of the last of the St Quintins.

THE END OF THE ESTATES?

It seems fitting to end with an estate like the Legards', which has all but disappeared, because all the old freehold estates in London (with the exception of the Queen's) are threatened with extinction. The menace comes from a piece of legislation called the Leasehold Reform, Housing and Urban Development Act 1993. The act sounds innocuous enough, but its consequences are potentially revolutionary. Under this act, all lease-holders in flats and houses have the right to buy their freeholds, subject to certain conditions. It remains to be seen how many of them will be either able or willing to exercise their new right, but if significant numbers of them do, the old estates will inevitably be broken up and will become yet another chapter in the long history of London.

There are those, such as the members of the Leasehold Enfranchisement Association, who think this may not be such a bad thing. Perhaps it is not, for the freeholders have benefited greatly from the increase in the value of their land over the centuries without actually putting anything into its development. In virtually every case, all the capital for building was provided by the house builders, many of whom went bust as a result. Maybe it is time, therefore, for the freeholders' free ride to come to an end.

TAKEN FOR GRANTED

Many features of London have become so familiar to us that we take them completely for granted. Sometimes they are conspicuous things, landmarks even, like Cleopatra's Needle or the BT Tower. Sometimes they are less obvious things like drinking fountains or blue plaques. Occasionally they are names, such as Dick Whittington's, that are indissolubly linked with the city. All of these features have fascinating but largely unknown stories behind them. Here, we recount a dozen of the most interesting of them in the hope that they will rescue their subjects from an unmerited, if understandable, neglect.

THE LIGHTS OF PICCADILLY CIRCUS

Piccadilly Circus, right in the heart of the capital, is a good place to start. This central hub is famous for its illuminated advertisements. The fronts of some buildings are now almost entirely covered by ever-changing walls of coloured lights spelling out the names of well-known products and even the temperature. But why are the lights there at all, and why are they only in one part of Piccadilly Circus?

Once upon a time Piccadilly Circus was a true circus, in other words a circular interchange linking the upper part of Regent Street with the lower part and Waterloo Place. Then in 1886 a new road was created leading off from the north-east. To improve access to this road – Shaftesbury Avenue – buildings on the south side of what is now Glasshouse Street were demolished, leaving the buildings on the north side facing directly on to the circus. The occupants of these buildings were suddenly presented with fantastic advertising possibilities. Taking advantage of the new technology of electrically illuminated advertisements, particularly the intermittent or flashing variety that attracted attention, some of them quickly put up large signs on the roofs of their buildings.

Vulgar additions

The London County Council disapproved of these vulgar additions to the London streetscape and succeeded in getting them removed. But its clever opponents countered by attaching the signs to the fronts of their buildings instead. The only way the council could have them removed now was by invoking by-laws concerned with the safety of pedestrians walking on the pavements below. It did try to apply these by-laws, but the courts ruled that the signs presented no danger to the public and could therefore stay. Thus by 1910 famous names like Bovril and Schweppes shone forth in illuminated coloured letters 8 feet (2.4 metres) high and there was nothing that anybody could do about it.

Meanwhile, on the triangular Trocadero site, now occupied by **Madame Tussaud's Rock Circus** among others things, the council was itself the freeholder, so here it could apply not only by-laws but the clauses of its own leases to attack the new signs. The trouble was its leases had been drafted long before anyone had even heard of illuminated advertisements, and the wording wasn't specific enough to deal with the new situation. So although the council succeeded in getting Mr Hutter of the Piccadilly Restaurant on the top floor to take down a Gordon's Gin sign because its fixings damaged the façade of the building, it was powerless when the ingenious restaurateur simply constructed a steel frame protruding out over the roof parapet and hung the sign on it clear of the façade! By the early 1920s the battle of the lights had been won by the advertisers. Looking back, their victory would have been achieved much sooner had it not been for the austerity brought by the First World War.

If you go to Piccadilly Circus today, you will see that the lights – the subject of countless picture postcards – are concentrated in one section of the circus. The simple reason for this is that the freehold of the rest of the circus is owned by the Crown Estate. Like the old London County Council, the Crown Estate was opposed to the signs, but it had the advantage of better leases which could be, and since have been, successfully enforced to prevent the erection of any signs of which it disapproves. For this reason there have never been any illuminated advertisements on Crown buildings, and, according to recent pronouncements, there never will be.

THE STATUE OF EROS

Piccadilly Circus's other claim to fame is the statue of Eros. This is a misnomer for two reasons. First, it is not a statue at all but a memorial fountain commemorating the great Victorian philanthropist, the Earl of Shaftesbury, after whom Shaftesbury Avenue is named. Second, the figure so delicately poised atop the fountain is not the God of Love but the Angel of Christian Charity. At least, that is what the experts say. The situation is confused somewhat by the words of the sculptor himself, Sir Arthur Gilbert, who said that the naked figure (formerly golden, now leaden and not the original) represents 'the blindfolded love sending forth ... his missile of kindness'. It would seem therefore that Gilbert did indeed create the figure to represent love, but the love he had in mind was a religious sort, not the erotic type suggested both by the resemblance of the figure to Cupid and by the popular christening of the memorial 'the statue of Eros' within a fortnight of its unveiling in June 1893.

Rancour

Given the nature of Lord Shaftesbury's work, it is extraordinary how much rancour his memorial managed to excite. Interference with the design by both the Memorial Committee and the London County Council led to squabbles between the two bodies and even more bitter arguments between them and the ultra-sensitive Gilbert. Gilbert was particularly incensed by the council's insistence that he reduce the size of the main fountain basin. The memorial was also meant to function as a public drinking fountain, and Gilbert claimed that, if the basin were made too small, drinkers would get soaked in their attempts to get a drink of water. After the unveiling (which he refused to attend) he was proved right and was pilloried for it in the press, even though he was in no way to blame. With his public reputation temporarily in shreds, he was also nearly bankrupt because the bronze had cost him far more than he had estimated. It comes as no surprise to find Gilbert admitting many years later that the Shaftesbury memorial affair traumatized his entire life.

Had the memorial been constructed to Gilbert's design, it would be a much more exciting structure than the rather dismal stump it is today. Not only would there be a large fountain playing into a wide basin at ground level, but the fountains at the top would form a shimmering globe of water, above which the graceful angel would appear to be hovering, completely unsupported.

There is one final intriguing mystery about Eros. Is the statue a clever pun on Shaftesbury's name? If you look closely at Eros's bow, you will notice that it has no arrow in it and that it is pointing downwards. Are we meant to conjecture from this that the arrow or 'shaft' has been fired downwards and that it now lies 'buried' in the ground? There would certainly appear to be some kind of connection, but whether Gilbert ever intended it or not we shall never know for sure.

DRINKING FOUNTAINS

All over central London, in parks and gardens and by the sides of roads, you will find public drinking fountains. Many bear the name of one organization: the Metropolitan Drinking Fountain and Cattle Trough Association. Before this organization was founded in 1859, it was incredibly difficult – incredible in relation to our own experience today – for the vast majority of Londoners to get something as simple as a drink of water when they were out and about in the streets. Cart drivers and cabbies faced the additional difficulty of watering their horses. In fact the only places where horses could be watered were in the troughs some publicans placed outside their pubs. The water in these troughs was not free, however. It had to be paid for, either directly or by buying beer. 'All that water their horses here/Must pay a penny or have some beer' was one common sign erected above many public houses' water troughs. With 50,000-plus horses on the streets at any one time, horse-watering must have been a lucrative business for the average publican.

By the mid-1850s some improvements had been effected in the supply of drinking water to the capital, but distribution was still woefully inadequate. Into the breach stepped Samuel Gurney, MP and member of a well-known Quaker banking and philanthropic family. Through his efforts the Metropolitan Free Drinking Fountain Association was set up on 10 April 1859. Just 11 days later the first drinking fountain, incorporating its own filtration system, was activated in front of a large crowd of eager onlookers. The fountain, paid for by Gurney, was let into the wall of St Sepulchre's Church in Newgate Street and can still be seen there today, complete with its two metal drinking cups (see page 156).

Bowls for dogs

Over the next couple of years more fountains were installed at the rate of nearly one a week. Before long, most incorporated small bowls for dogs. Then the association decided to tackle the horse problem, too: in 1867 it changed its name to include cattle troughs ('cattle' was used rather than 'horse' because the troughs were also intended for live cattle on their way to market) and started installing these all over London. The ones we see today are the solid granite variety introduced after the first metal ones had proved unsatisfactory. The association continued installing troughs until the 1950s, when horse-drawn traffic was finally driven off the roads by motorized transport.

Today the association, which is based in Chislehurst in Kent, continues to install modern drinking fountains in schools and playing fields and also helps people in other countries, notably Africa, obtain their own supplies of fresh drinking water. Meanwhile its older fountains in London present a pretty sorry sight. Few work, and most are filled with rubbish. This isn't the fault of the association. The responsibility for maintaining fountains lies with local authorities. Unfortunately, they are often hamstrung by a lack of resources – and in an age when most people can either turn on a tap or buy a bottle of mineral water, the renovation of derelict public drinking fountains is not a high priority.

CABBIES' SHELTERS

One inclement day in 1874 Captain George Armstrong, late of the army of the East India Company and now managing editor of the *Globe* newspaper, wanted to take a cab. Although there were cabs on the stand, none of the drivers were to be seen. After a bit of searching Armstrong discovered them in the local pub. They were naturally sheltering from the weather and at the same time enjoying some refreshment, primarily alcoholic. How much better it would be, he thought, if cabbies didn't have to go to pubs in bad weather. With their own refreshment rooms, they could get cheaper food and would be protected from the temptations of drink. Victorian cabmen were notorious for their drunkenness.

So was born the Cabmen's Shelter Fund, an organization dedicated to building alcohol-free shelters for cab drivers complete with tables and benches and kitchens for cooking meals. Between 1875 and 1914, 61 shelters were built. Today 13 survive, five of them in Belgravia and Kensington, then as now smart residential suburbs and therefore the sorts of places where many cab journeys would start or end. The shelters look like rather grand garden sheds, a resemblance reinforced by their smart green livery. The Belgravia shelters are in Grosvenor Gardens and Pont Street. The Kensington shelters are in Kensington Road near the junction with Gloucester Road, Thurloe Place by the Victoria & Albert Museum, and Kensington Park Road just off Notting Hill Gate. Recently restored, these and the other surviving shelters are all still used by cab drivers. The Transport and General Workers Union administers the Cabmen's Shelter Fund and collects its small annual income from the licence fees paid by cab drivers.

THE COADE STONE LION

A London landmark no doubt well known to cabbies is the magnificent lion guarding the entrance to Westminster Bridge opposite the Houses of Parliament. This noble beast is not the stone sculpture you might think it is from a casual glance, but a piece of pottery made from a mould and fired in a kiln. It is, moreover, over 160 years old, yet it shows not a trace of its age, a testimony to the strength and weather-resistant property of the material from which it is made. This material is an artificial stone called Coade stone, named after its inventor, Eleanor Coade. Born in Exeter in

Opposite: The splendid Coade stone lion was made in 1837 according to a secret artificial stone formula rediscovered by the British Museum in the 1970s.